ANGEL ™

Surrogates

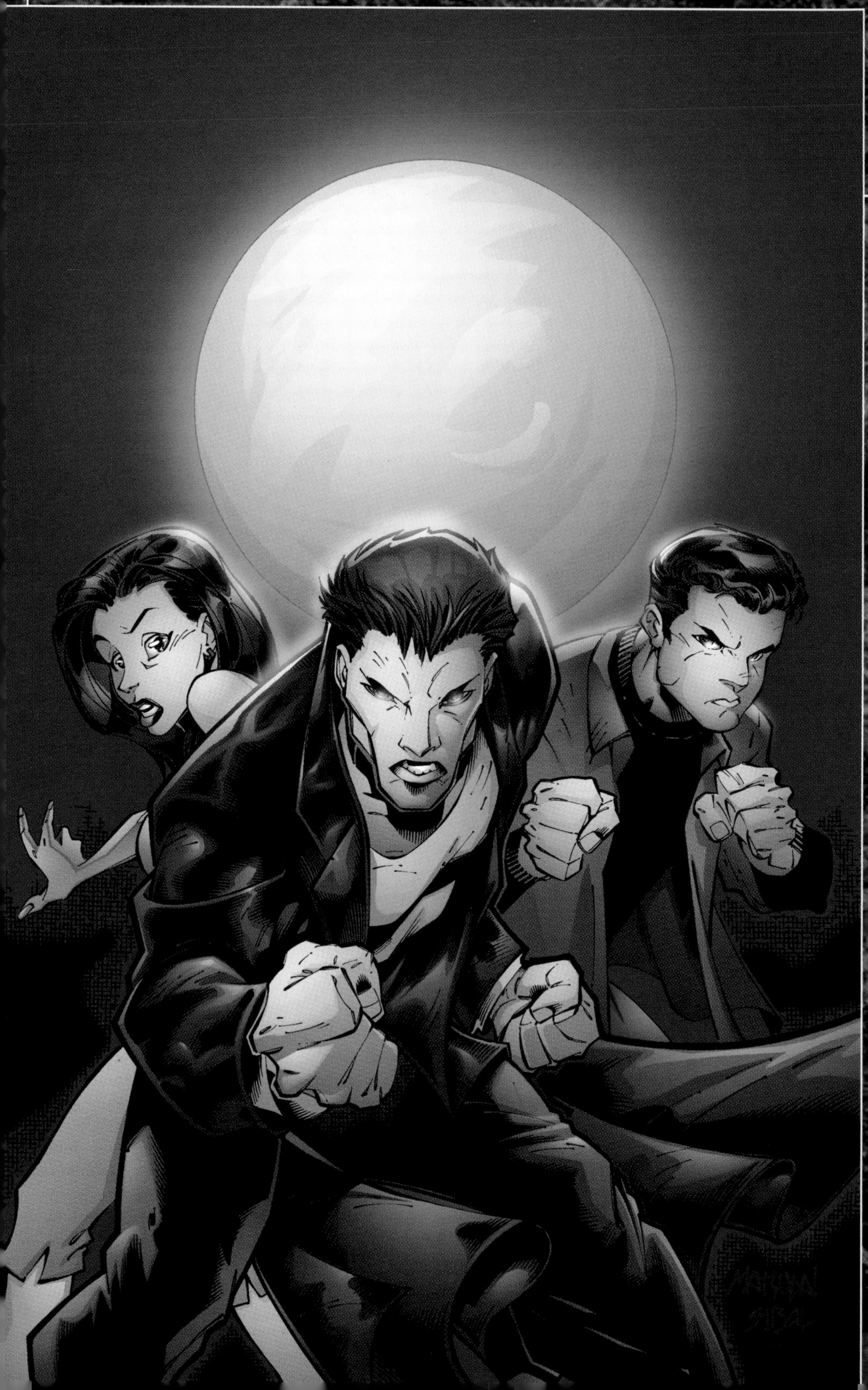

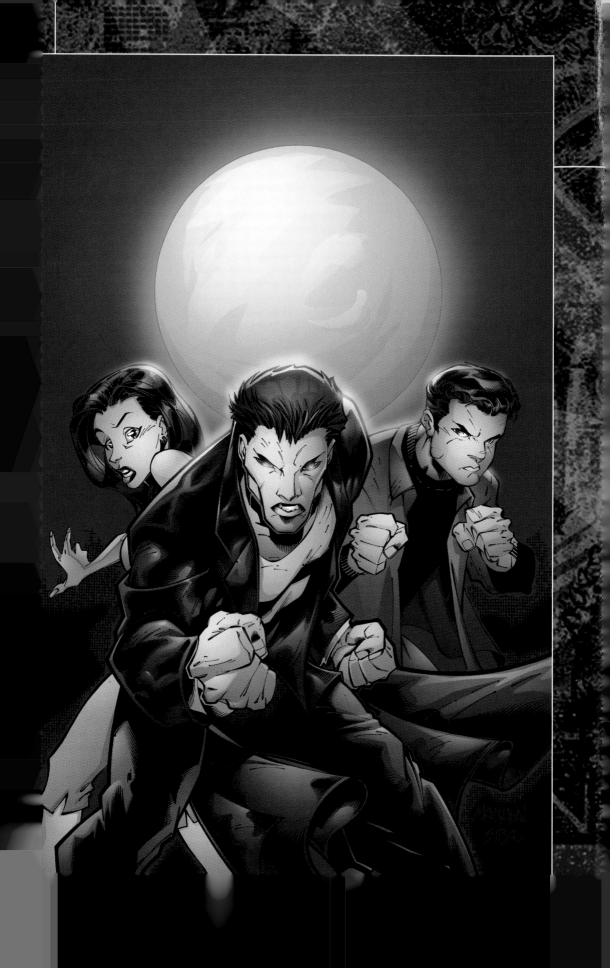

ANGEL ™

Surrogates

based on the television series
created by
JOSS WHEDON and DAVID GREENWALT

writer
CHRISTOPHER GOLDEN

penciller
CHRISTIAN ZANIER

pencil assists
MARVIN MARIANO

inker
ANDY OWENS
with JASON MINOR and CURTIS P. ARNOLD

colorist
GUY MAJOR

letterers
CLEM ROBINS and AMADOR CISNEROS

DARK HORSE COMICS

publisher
MIKE RICHARDSON

editor
SCOTT ALLIE
with ADAM GALLARDO

collection designer
KEITH WOOD

art director
MARK COX

Special thanks to
DEBBIE OLSHAN at Fox Licensing,
CAROLINE KALLAS and GEORGE SNYDER at
Buffy the Vampire Slayer.

Published by
Dark Horse Comics, Inc.
10956 SE Main Street
Milwaukie, OR 97222

First edition: December 2000
ISBN: 1-56971-491-6

1 3 5 7 9 10 8 6 4 2

Printed in Canada.

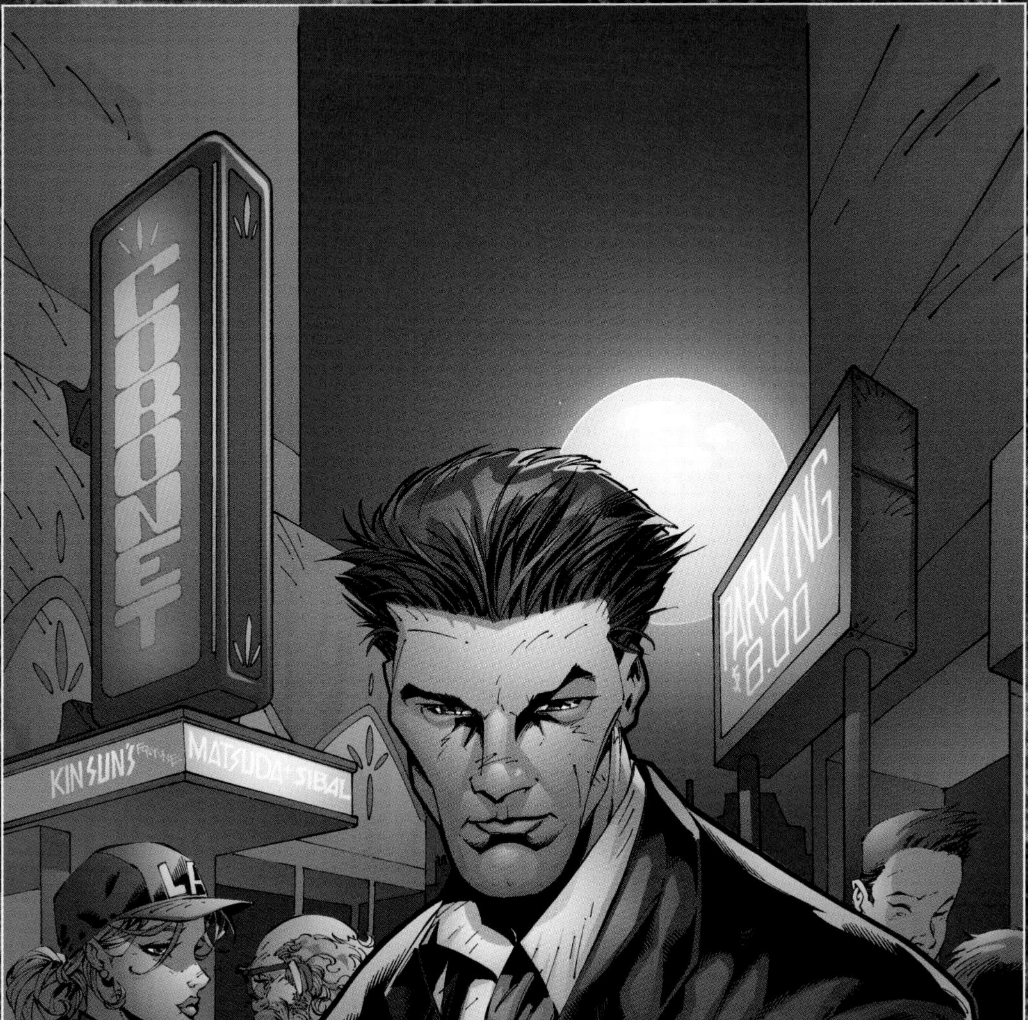
CORONET
KIN SUN'S
MATSUDA & SIBAL
LA
PARKING
$8.00

Cover by **JEFF MATSUDA** and **JON SIBAL**
Colors by **GUY MAJOR**

Surrogates
Chapter 1

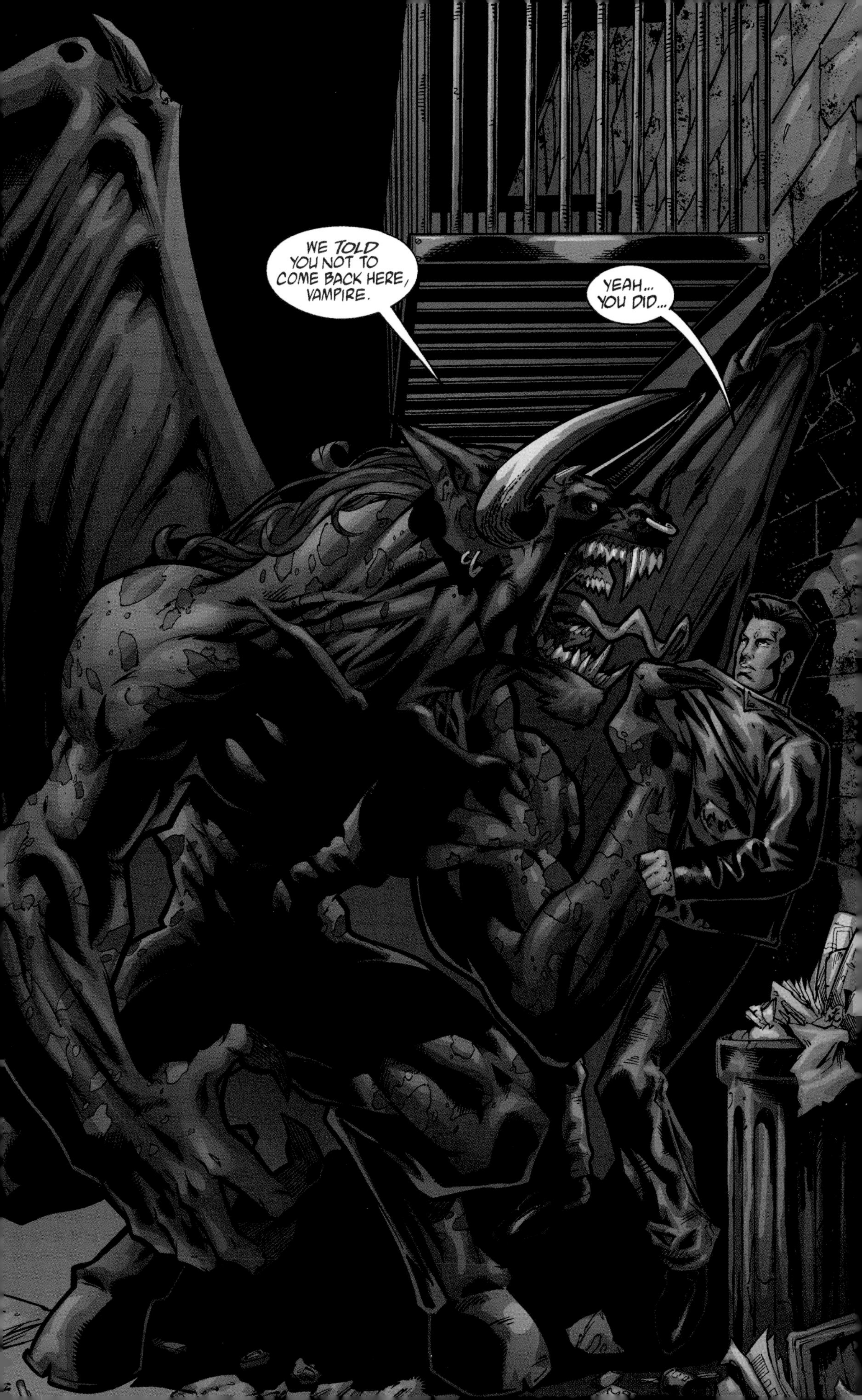
WE TOLD YOU NOT TO COME BACK HERE, VAMPIRE.
YEAH... YOU DID...

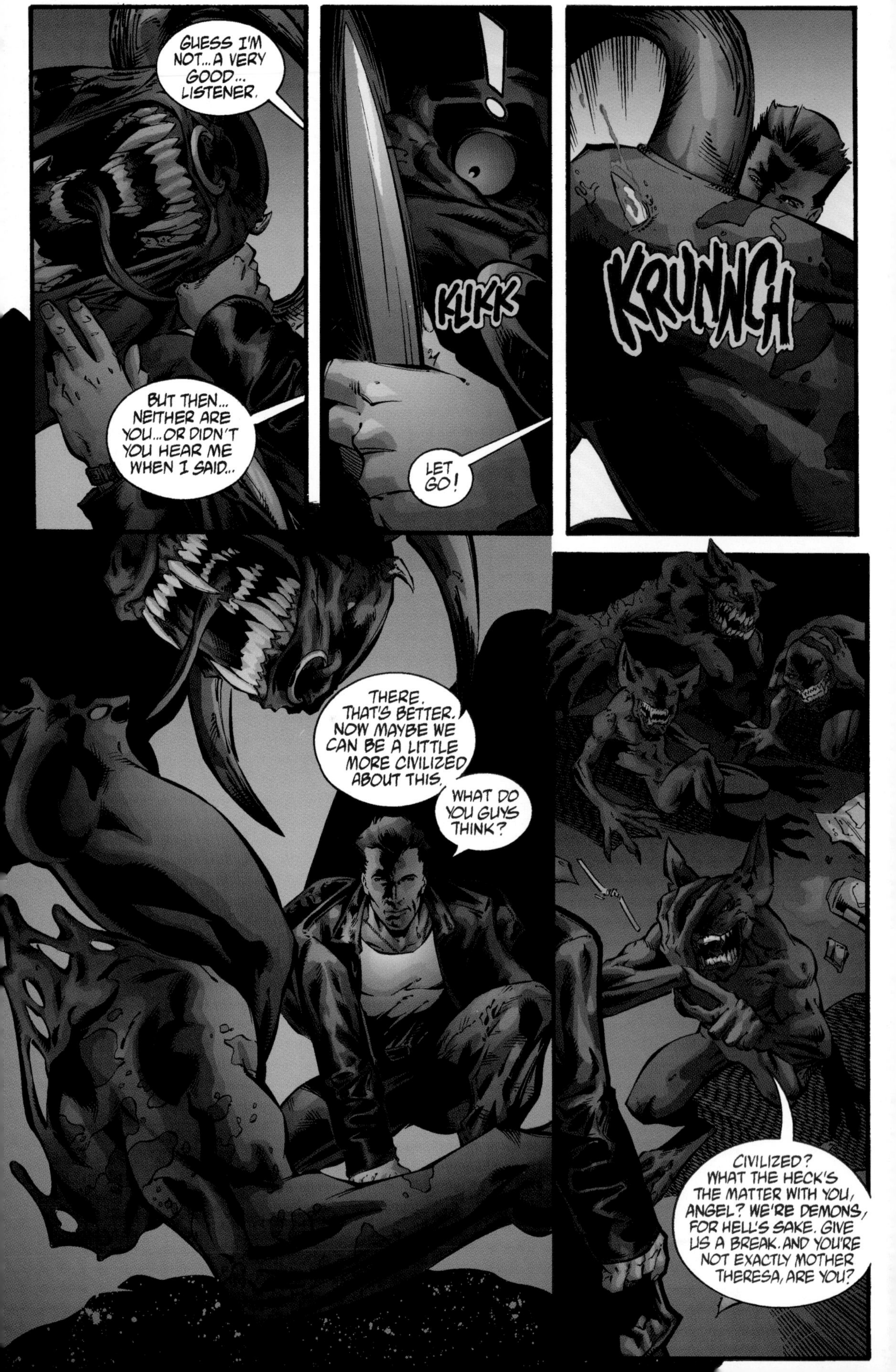
GUESS I'M NOT...A VERY GOOD... LISTENER.
BUT THEN... NEITHER ARE YOU...OR DIDN'T YOU HEAR ME WHEN I SAID...
KLIKK
LET GO!
KRUNNCH
THERE. THAT'S BETTER. NOW MAYBE WE CAN BE A LITTLE MORE CIVILIZED ABOUT THIS.
WHAT DO YOU GUYS THINK?
CIVILIZED? WHAT THE HECK'S THE MATTER WITH YOU, ANGEL? WE'RE DEMONS, FOR HELL'S SAKE. GIVE US A BREAK. AND YOU'RE NOT EXACTLY MOTHER THERESA, ARE YOU?

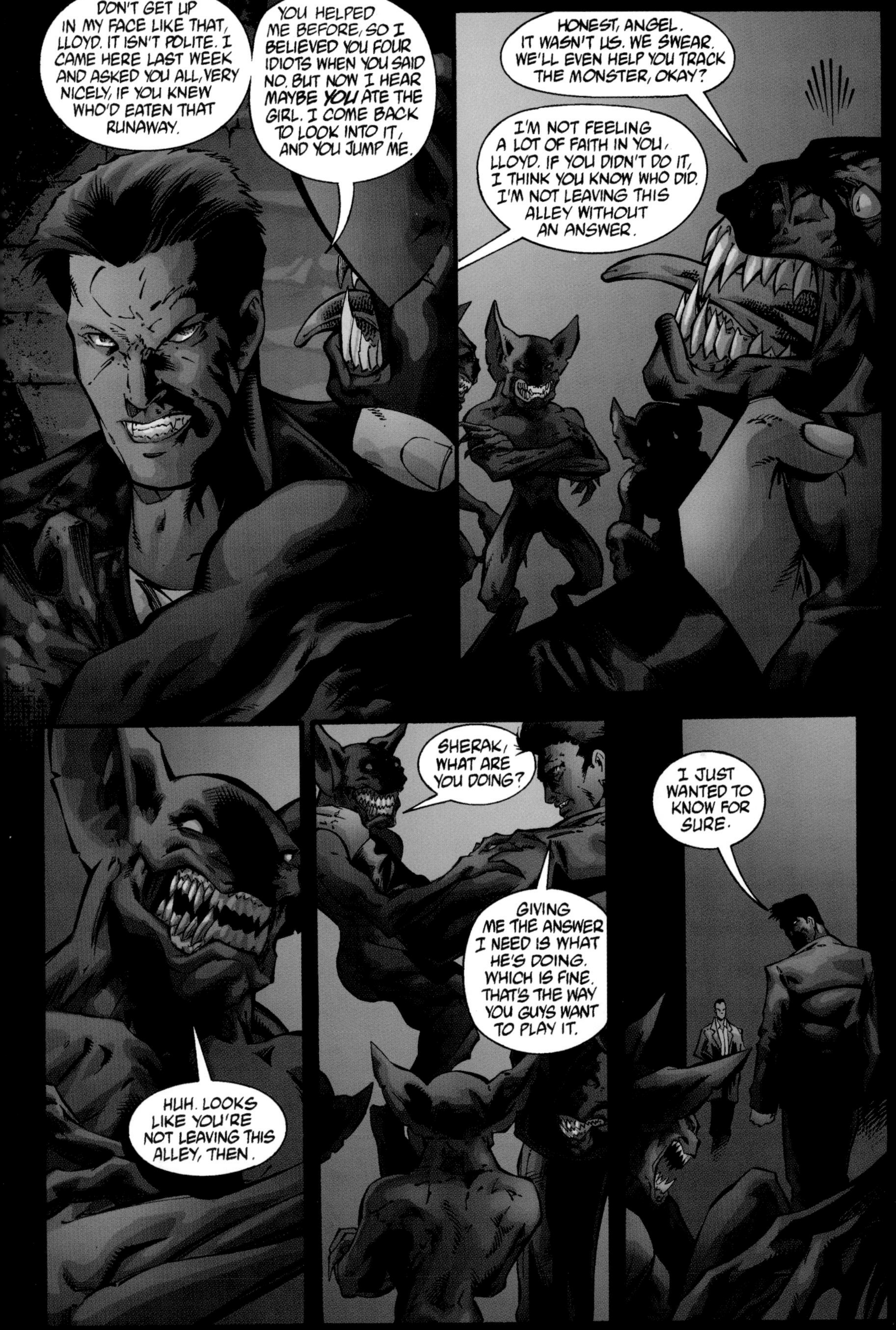
DON'T GET UP IN MY FACE LIKE THAT, LLOYD. IT ISN'T POLITE. I CAME HERE LAST WEEK AND ASKED YOU ALL, VERY NICELY, IF YOU KNEW WHO'D EATEN THAT RUNAWAY.
YOU HELPED ME BEFORE, SO I BELIEVED YOU FOUR IDIOTS WHEN YOU SAID NO. BUT NOW I HEAR MAYBE YOU ATE THE GIRL. I COME BACK TO LOOK INTO IT, AND YOU JUMP ME.
HONEST, ANGEL. IT WASN'T US. WE SWEAR. WE'LL EVEN HELP YOU TRACK THE MONSTER, OKAY?
I'M NOT FEELING A LOT OF FAITH IN YOU, LLOYD. IF YOU DIDN'T DO IT, I THINK YOU KNOW WHO DID. I'M NOT LEAVING THIS ALLEY WITHOUT AN ANSWER.
HUH. LOOKS LIKE YOU'RE NOT LEAVING THIS ALLEY, THEN.
SHERAK, WHAT ARE YOU DOING?
GIVING ME THE ANSWER I NEED IS WHAT HE'S DOING. WHICH IS FINE. THAT'S THE WAY YOU GUYS WANT TO PLAY IT.
I JUST WANTED TO KNOW FOR SURE.

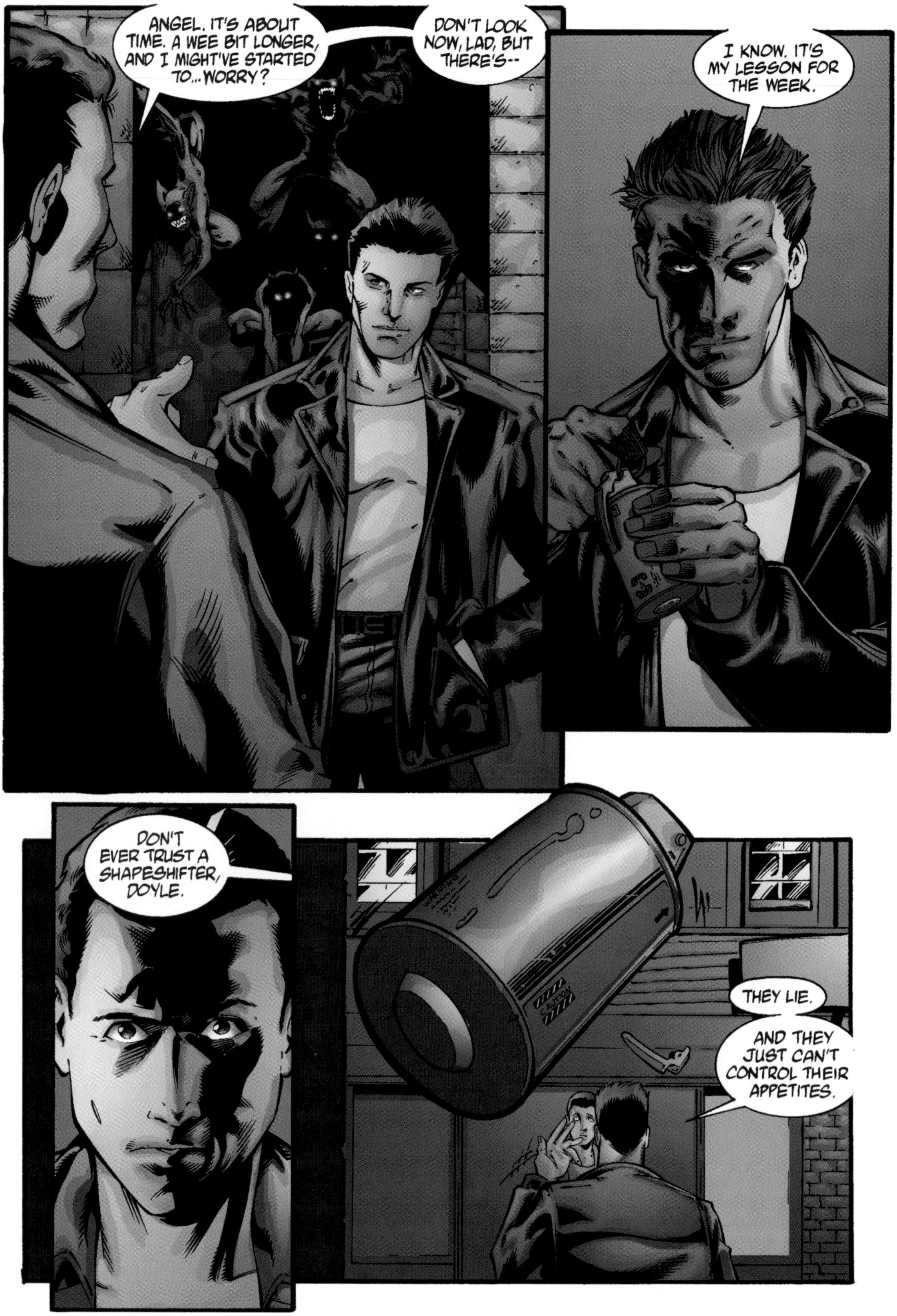
ANGEL. IT'S ABOUT TIME. A WEE BIT LONGER, AND I MIGHT'VE STARTED TO... WORRY?
DON'T LOOK NOW, LAD, BUT THERE'S--
I KNOW. IT'S MY LESSON FOR THE WEEK.
DON'T EVER TRUST A SHAPESHIFTER, DOYLE.
THEY LIE.
AND THEY JUST CAN'T CONTROL THEIR APPETITES.

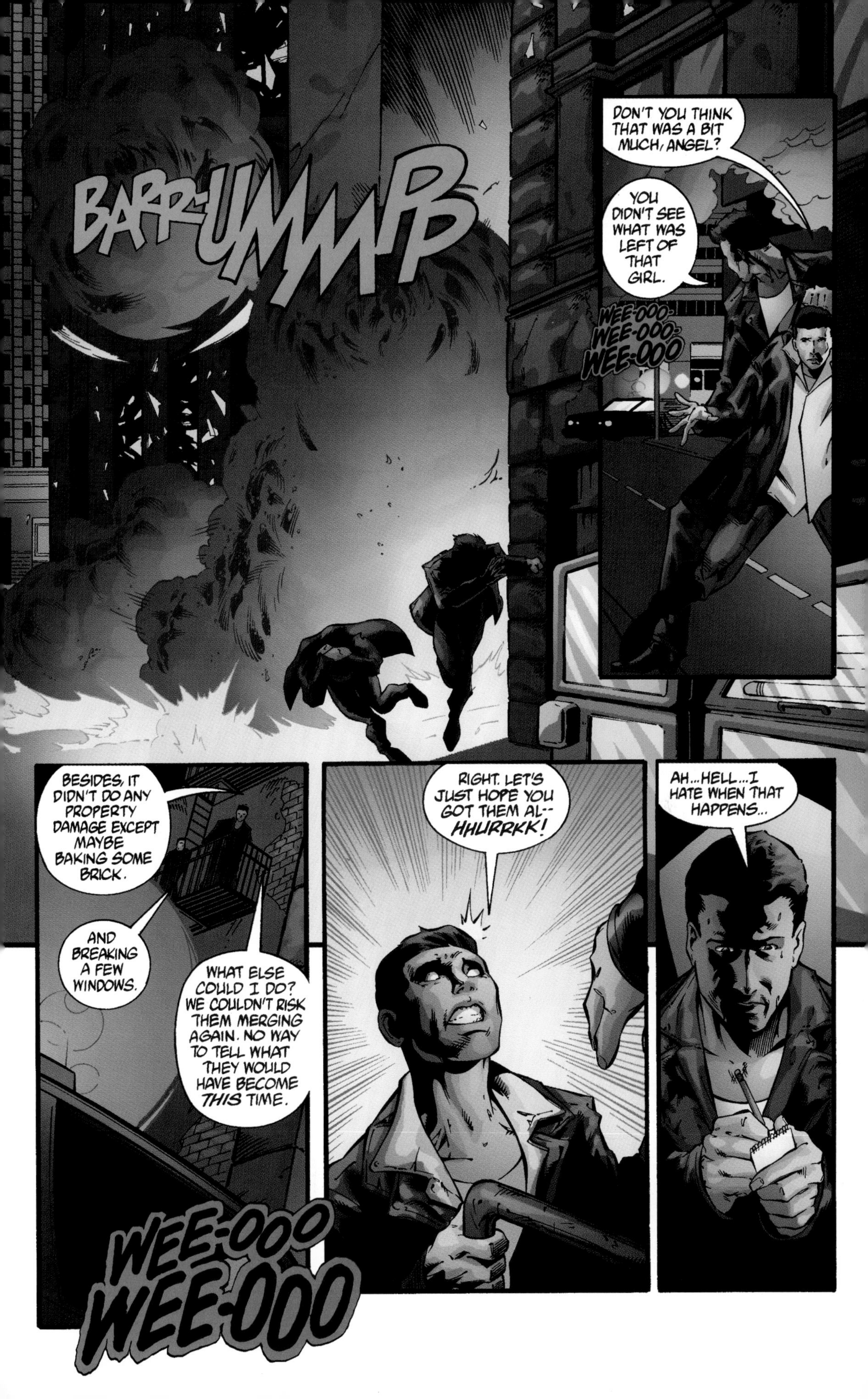
BARR-UMMPB
DON'T YOU THINK THAT WAS A BIT MUCH, ANGEL?
YOU DIDN'T SEE WHAT WAS LEFT OF THAT GIRL.
WEE-OOO-WEE-OOO-WEE-OOO
BESIDES, IT DIDN'T DO ANY PROPERTY DAMAGE EXCEPT MAYBE BAKING SOME BRICK.
AND BREAKING A FEW WINDOWS.
WHAT ELSE COULD I DO? WE COULDN'T RISK THEM MERGING AGAIN. NO WAY TO TELL WHAT THEY WOULD HAVE BECOME *THIS* TIME.
RIGHT. LET'S JUST HOPE YOU GOT THEM AL-- *HHURRKK!*
AH...HELL...I HATE WHEN THAT HAPPENS...
WEE-OOO WEE-OOO

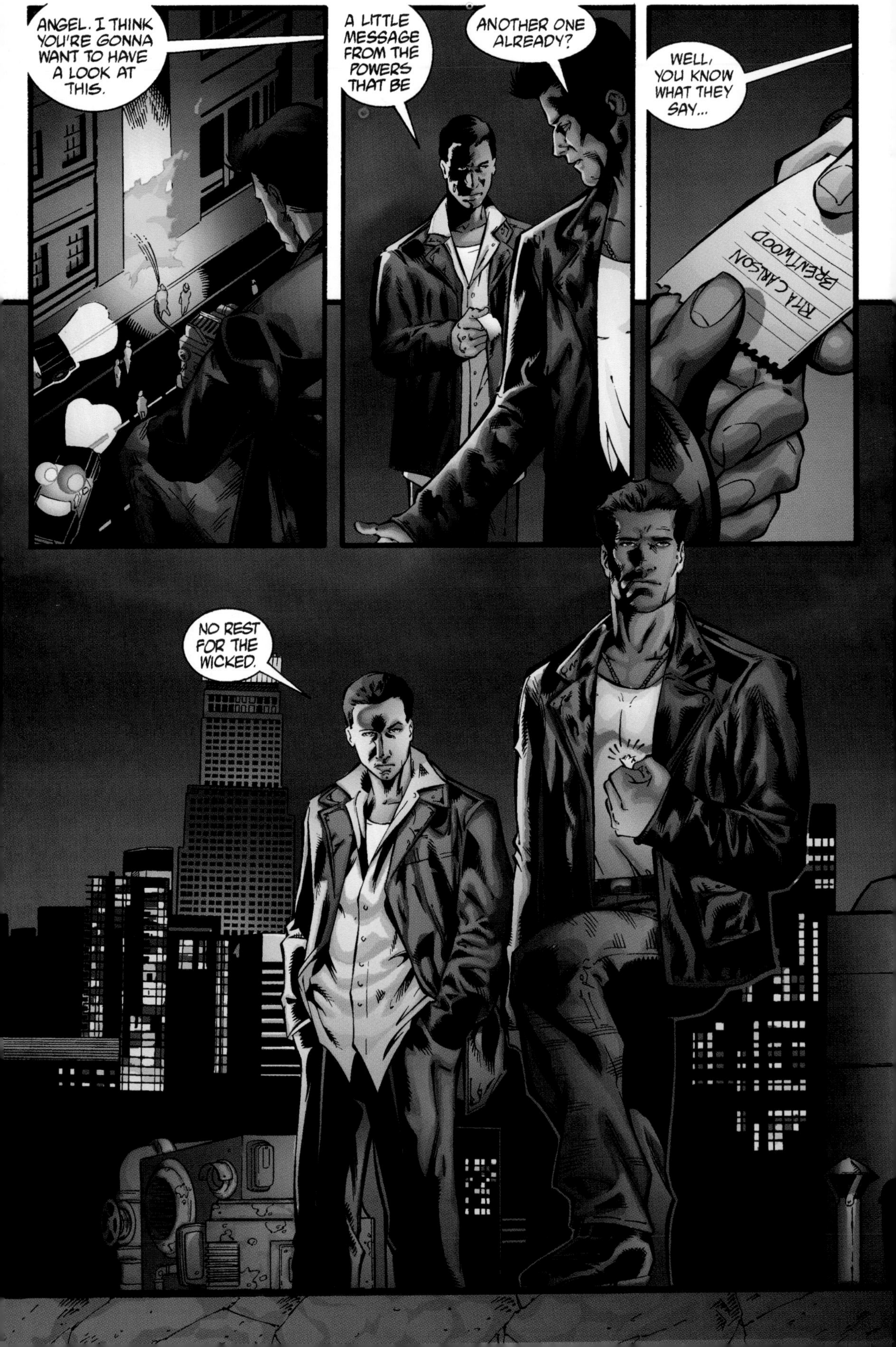
ANGEL. I THINK YOU'RE GONNA WANT TO HAVE A LOOK AT THIS.
A LITTLE MESSAGE FROM THE POWERS THAT BE
ANOTHER ONE ALREADY?
WELL, YOU KNOW WHAT THEY SAY...
RITA CARLSON
BRENTWOOD
NO REST FOR THE WICKED.

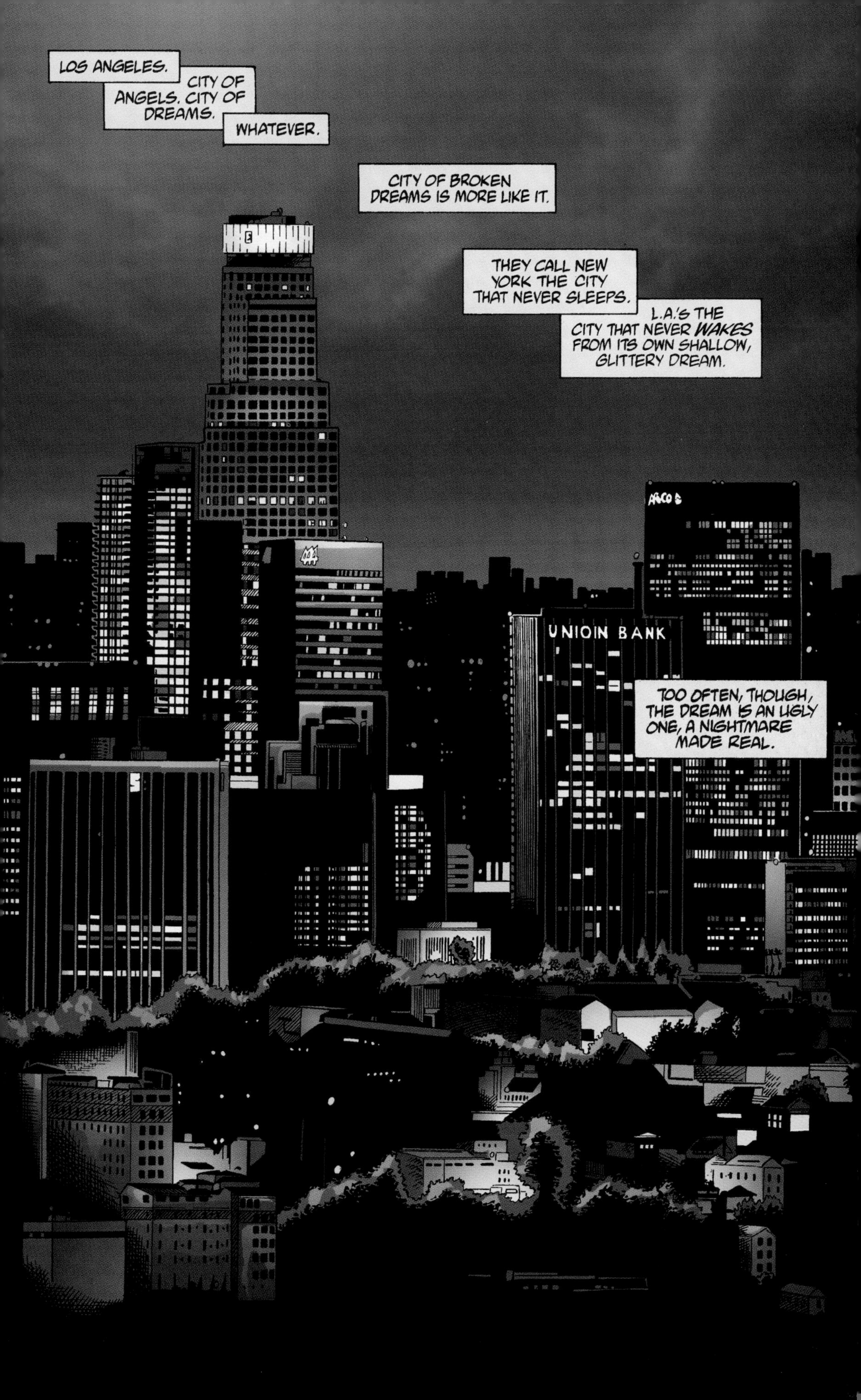
LOS ANGELES.
CITY OF ANGELS. CITY OF DREAMS.
WHATEVER.
CITY OF BROKEN DREAMS IS MORE LIKE IT.
THEY CALL NEW YORK THE CITY THAT NEVER SLEEPS.
L.A.'S THE CITY THAT NEVER WAKES FROM ITS OWN SHALLOW, GLITTERY DREAM.
UNION BANK
TOO OFTEN, THOUGH, THE DREAM IS AN UGLY ONE, A NIGHTMARE MADE REAL.

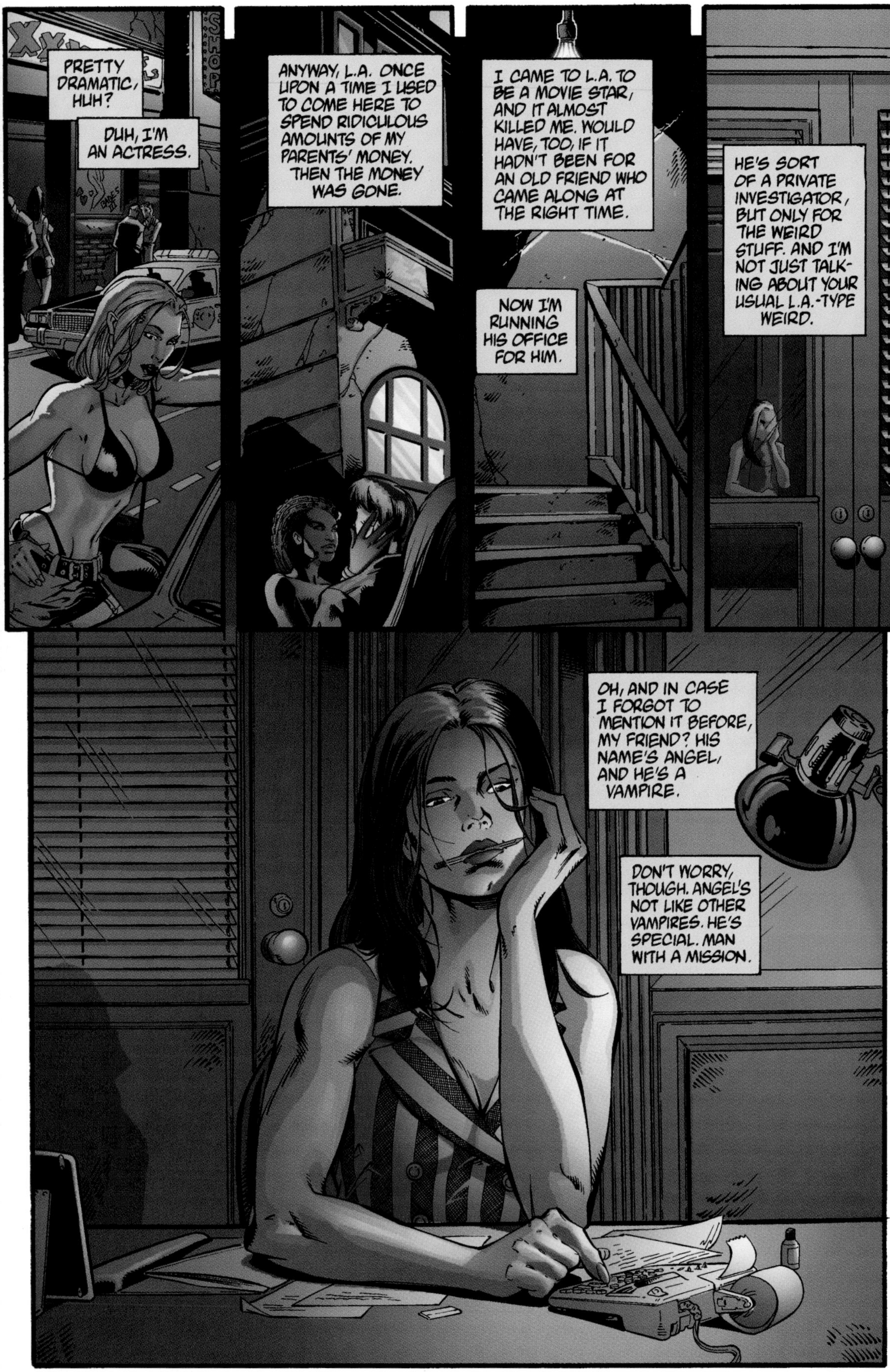
PRETTY DRAMATIC, HUH?
DUH, I'M AN ACTRESS.
ANYWAY, L.A. ONCE UPON A TIME I USED TO COME HERE TO SPEND RIDICULOUS AMOUNTS OF MY PARENTS' MONEY. THEN THE MONEY WAS GONE.
I CAME TO L.A. TO BE A MOVIE STAR, AND IT ALMOST KILLED ME. WOULD HAVE, TOO, IF IT HADN'T BEEN FOR AN OLD FRIEND WHO CAME ALONG AT THE RIGHT TIME.
NOW I'M RUNNING HIS OFFICE FOR HIM.
HE'S SORT OF A PRIVATE INVESTIGATOR, BUT ONLY FOR THE WEIRD STUFF. AND I'M NOT JUST TALKING ABOUT YOUR USUAL L.A.-TYPE WEIRD.
OH, AND IN CASE I FORGOT TO MENTION IT BEFORE, MY FRIEND? HIS NAME'S ANGEL, AND HE'S A VAMPIRE.
DON'T WORRY, THOUGH. ANGEL'S NOT LIKE OTHER VAMPIRES. HE'S SPECIAL. MAN WITH A MISSION.

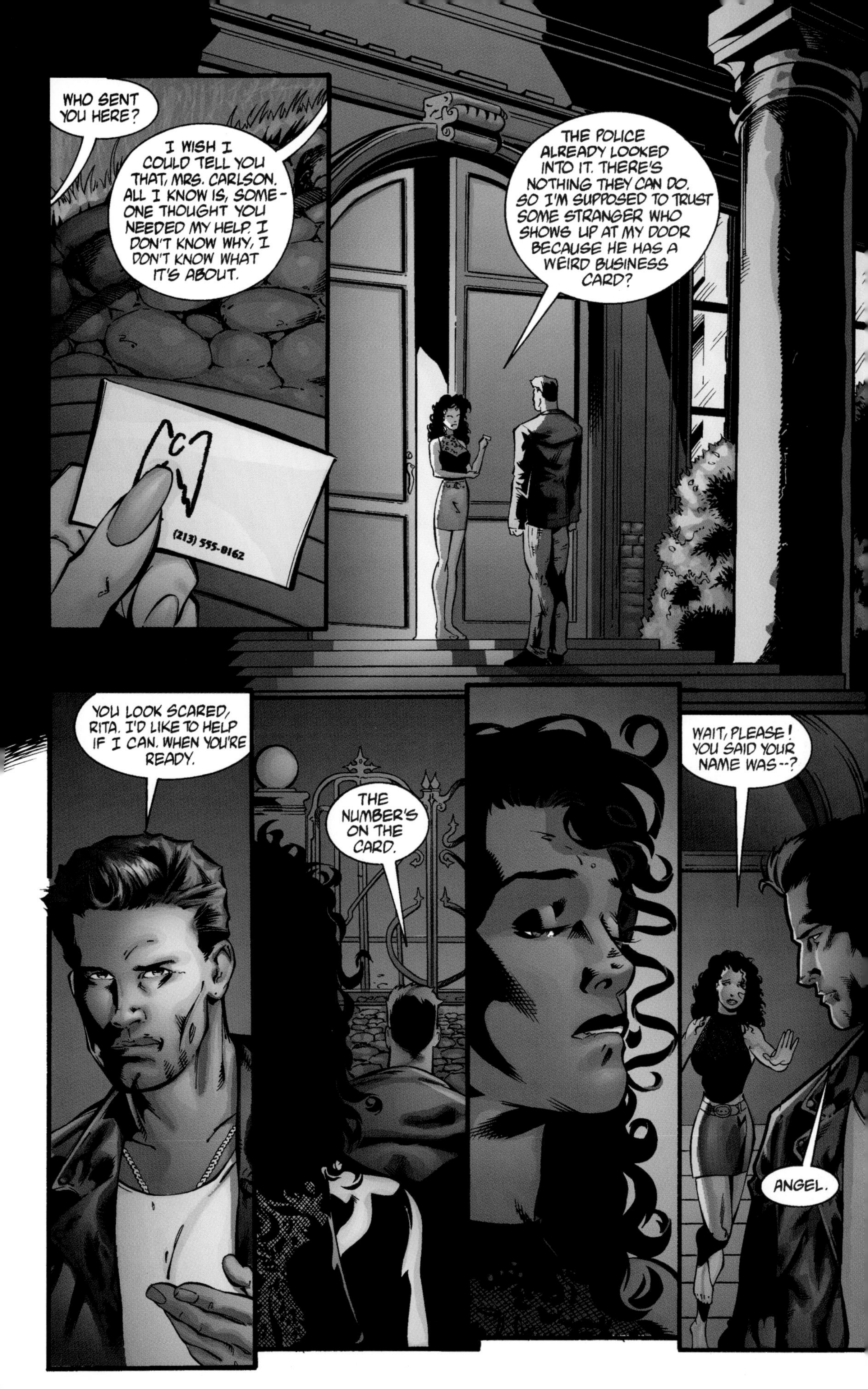
WHO SENT YOU HERE?
I WISH I COULD TELL YOU THAT, MRS. CARLSON. ALL I KNOW IS, SOME-ONE THOUGHT YOU NEEDED MY HELP. I DON'T KNOW WHY, I DON'T KNOW WHAT IT'S ABOUT.
(213) 555-8162
THE POLICE ALREADY LOOKED INTO IT. THERE'S NOTHING THEY CAN DO. SO I'M SUPPOSED TO TRUST SOME STRANGER WHO SHOWS UP AT MY DOOR BECAUSE HE HAS A WEIRD BUSINESS CARD?
YOU LOOK SCARED, RITA. I'D LIKE TO HELP IF I CAN. WHEN YOU'RE READY.
THE NUMBER'S ON THE CARD.
WAIT, PLEASE! YOU SAID YOUR NAME WAS--?
ANGEL.

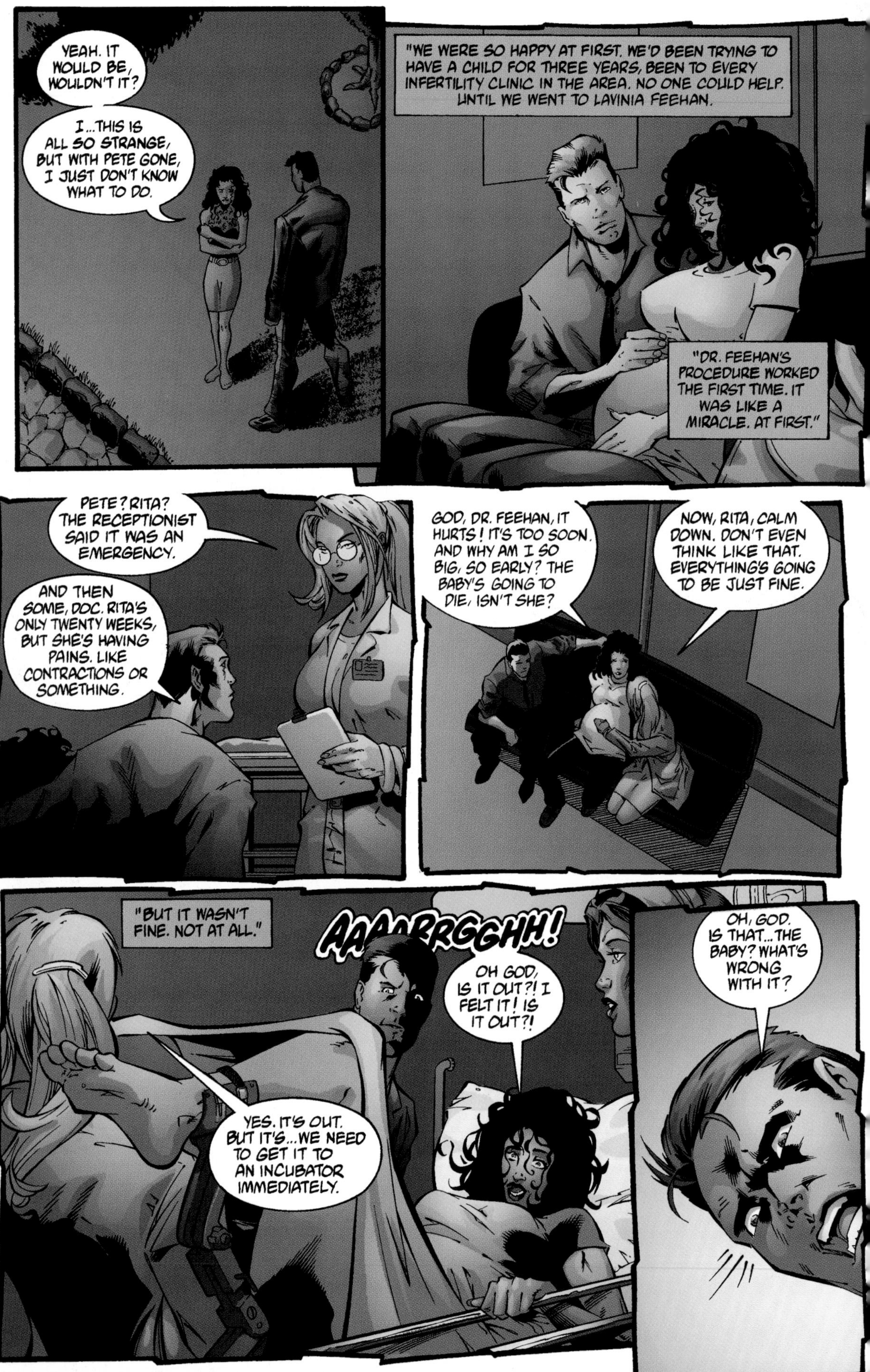
YEAH. IT WOULD BE, WOULDN'T IT?
I...THIS IS ALL SO STRANGE, BUT WITH PETE GONE, I JUST DON'T KNOW WHAT TO DO.
"WE WERE SO HAPPY AT FIRST. WE'D BEEN TRYING TO HAVE A CHILD FOR THREE YEARS, BEEN TO EVERY INFERTILITY CLINIC IN THE AREA. NO ONE COULD HELP. UNTIL WE WENT TO LAVINIA FEEHAN.
"DR. FEEHAN'S PROCEDURE WORKED THE FIRST TIME. IT WAS LIKE A MIRACLE. AT FIRST."
PETE? RITA? THE RECEPTIONIST SAID IT WAS AN EMERGENCY.
AND THEN SOME, DOC. RITA'S ONLY TWENTY WEEKS, BUT SHE'S HAVING PAINS. LIKE CONTRACTIONS OR SOMETHING.
GOD, DR. FEEHAN, IT HURTS! IT'S TOO SOON. AND WHY AM I SO BIG, SO EARLY? THE BABY'S GOING TO DIE, ISN'T SHE?
NOW, RITA, CALM DOWN. DON'T EVEN THINK LIKE THAT. EVERYTHING'S GOING TO BE JUST FINE.
"BUT IT WASN'T FINE. NOT AT ALL."
AAAARRGGHH!
OH GOD, IS IT OUT?! I FELT IT! IS IT OUT?!
YES. IT'S OUT. BUT IT'S...WE NEED TO GET IT TO AN INCUBATOR IMMEDIATELY.
OH, GOD. IS THAT...THE BABY? WHAT'S WRONG WITH IT?

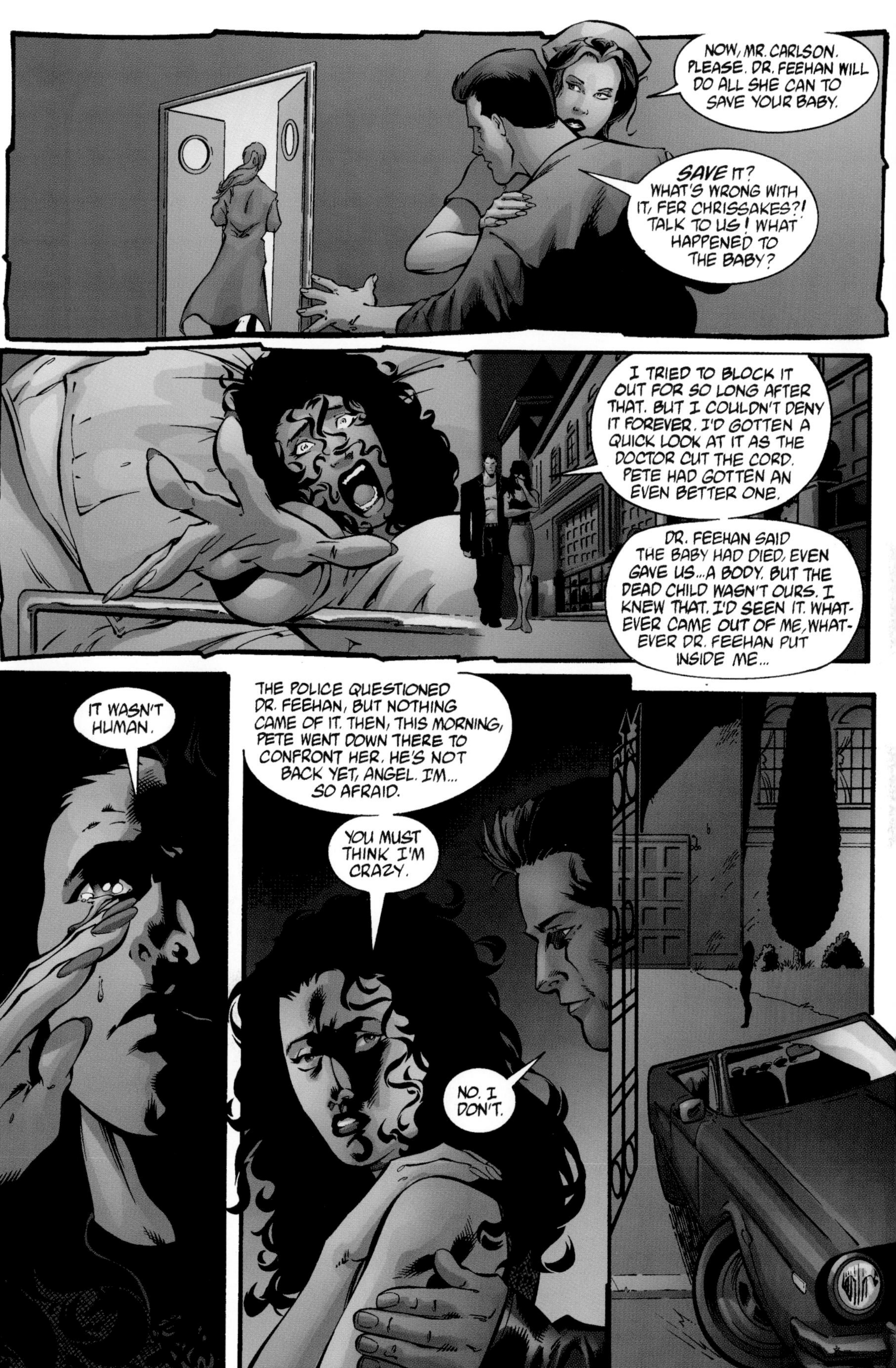
NOW, MR. CARLSON. PLEASE. DR. FEEHAN WILL DO ALL SHE CAN TO SAVE YOUR BABY.
SAVE IT? WHAT'S WRONG WITH IT, FER CHRISSAKES?! TALK TO US! WHAT HAPPENED TO THE BABY?
I TRIED TO BLOCK IT OUT FOR SO LONG AFTER THAT. BUT I COULDN'T DENY IT FOREVER. I'D GOTTEN A QUICK LOOK AT IT AS THE DOCTOR CUT THE CORD. PETE HAD GOTTEN AN EVEN BETTER ONE.
DR. FEEHAN SAID THE BABY HAD DIED, EVEN GAVE US...A BODY. BUT THE DEAD CHILD WASN'T OURS. I KNEW THAT. I'D SEEN IT. WHATEVER CAME OUT OF ME, WHATEVER DR. FEEHAN PUT INSIDE ME...
IT WASN'T HUMAN.
THE POLICE QUESTIONED DR. FEEHAN, BUT NOTHING CAME OF IT. THEN, THIS MORNING, PETE WENT DOWN THERE TO CONFRONT HER. HE'S NOT BACK YET, ANGEL. I'M... SO AFRAID.
YOU MUST THINK I'M CRAZY.
NO. I DON'T.

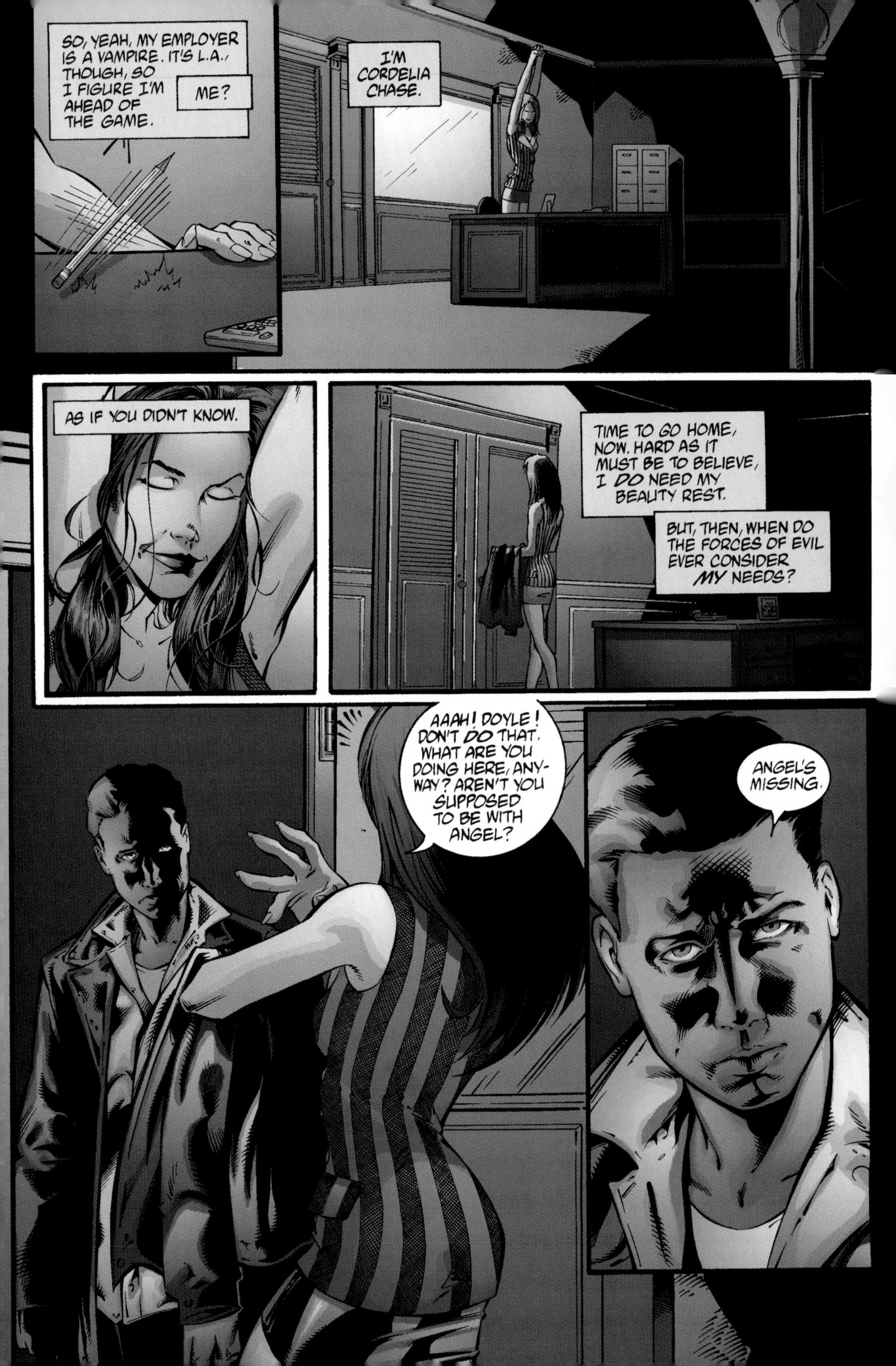
SO, YEAH, MY EMPLOYER IS A VAMPIRE. IT'S L.A., THOUGH, SO I FIGURE I'M AHEAD OF THE GAME.
ME?
I'M CORDELIA CHASE.
AS IF YOU DIDN'T KNOW.
TIME TO GO HOME, NOW. HARD AS IT MUST BE TO BELIEVE, I DO NEED MY BEAUTY REST.
BUT, THEN, WHEN DO THE FORCES OF EVIL EVER CONSIDER MY NEEDS?
AAAH! DOYLE! DON'T DO THAT. WHAT ARE YOU DOING HERE, ANYWAY? AREN'T YOU SUPPOSED TO BE WITH ANGEL?
ANGEL'S MISSING.

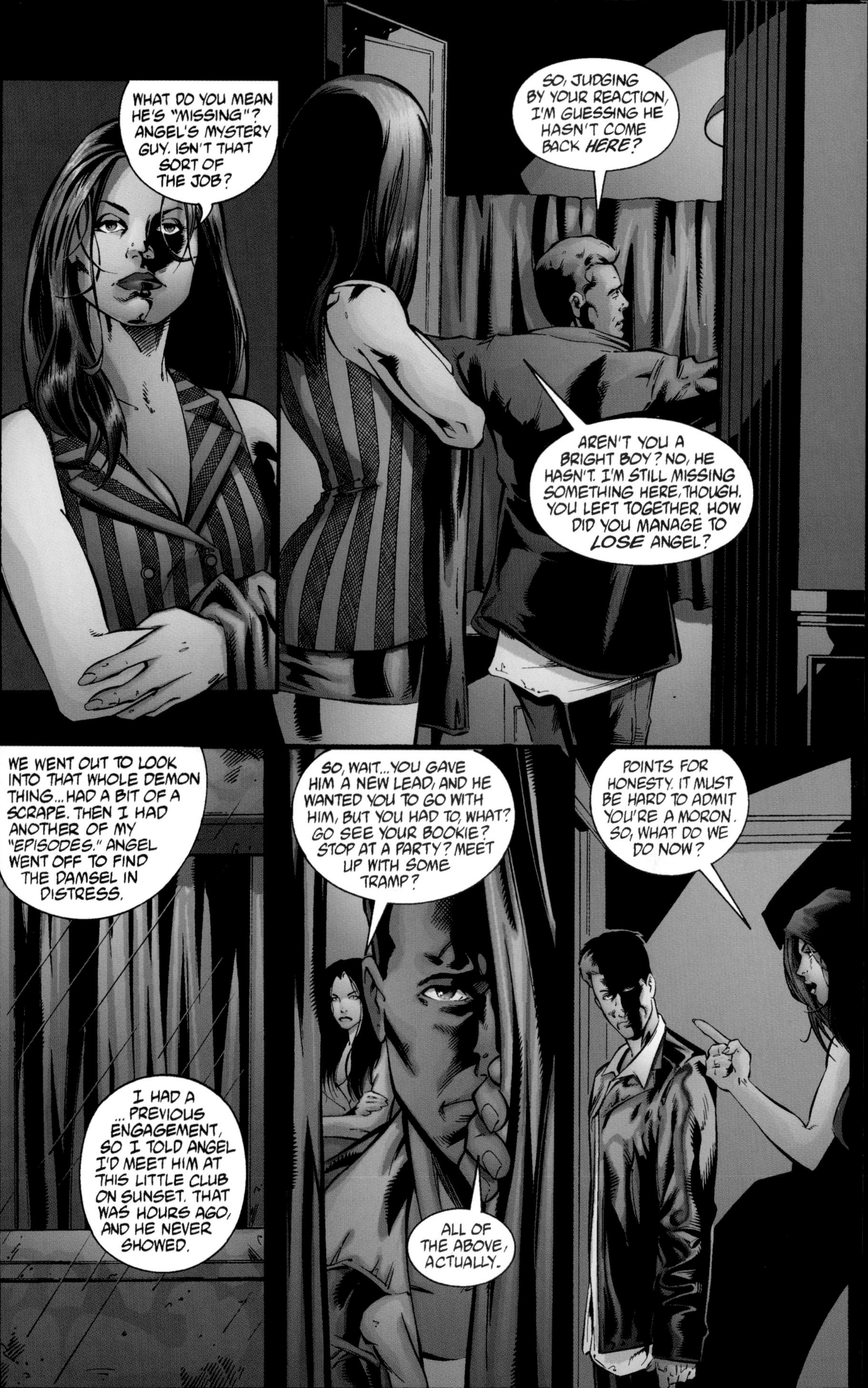
WHAT DO YOU MEAN HE'S "MISSING"? ANGEL'S MYSTERY GUY. ISN'T THAT SORT OF THE JOB?
SO, JUDGING BY YOUR REACTION, I'M GUESSING HE HASN'T COME BACK HERE?
AREN'T YOU A BRIGHT BOY? NO, HE HASN'T. I'M STILL MISSING SOMETHING HERE, THOUGH. YOU LEFT TOGETHER. HOW DID YOU MANAGE TO LOSE ANGEL?
WE WENT OUT TO LOOK INTO THAT WHOLE DEMON THING... HAD A BIT OF A SCRAPE. THEN I HAD ANOTHER OF MY "EPISODES." ANGEL WENT OFF TO FIND THE DAMSEL IN DISTRESS.
I HAD A ... PREVIOUS ENGAGEMENT, SO I TOLD ANGEL I'D MEET HIM AT THIS LITTLE CLUB ON SUNSET. THAT WAS HOURS AGO, AND HE NEVER SHOWED.
SO, WAIT... YOU GAVE HIM A NEW LEAD, AND HE WANTED YOU TO GO WITH HIM, BUT YOU HAD TO, WHAT? GO SEE YOUR BOOKIE? STOP AT A PARTY? MEET UP WITH SOME TRAMP?
ALL OF THE ABOVE, ACTUALLY.
POINTS FOR HONESTY. IT MUST BE HARD TO ADMIT YOU'RE A MORON. SO, WHAT DO WE DO NOW?

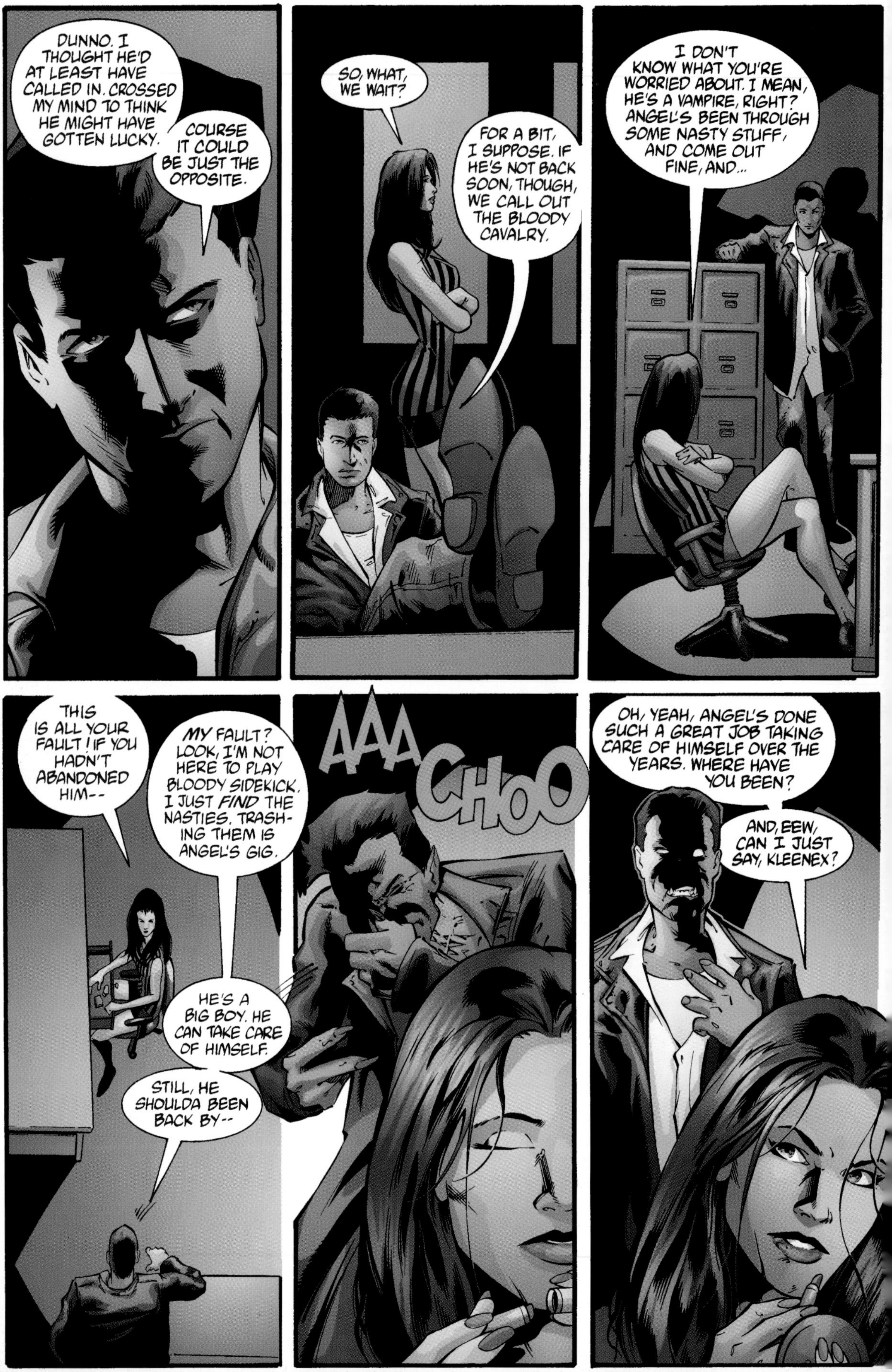
DUNNO. I THOUGHT HE'D AT LEAST HAVE CALLED IN. CROSSED MY MIND TO THINK HE MIGHT HAVE GOTTEN LUCKY.
COURSE IT COULD BE JUST THE OPPOSITE.
SO, WHAT, WE WAIT?
FOR A BIT, I SUPPOSE. IF HE'S NOT BACK SOON, THOUGH, WE CALL OUT THE BLOODY CAVALRY.
I DON'T KNOW WHAT YOU'RE WORRIED ABOUT. I MEAN, HE'S A VAMPIRE, RIGHT? ANGEL'S BEEN THROUGH SOME NASTY STUFF, AND COME OUT FINE, AND...
THIS IS ALL YOUR FAULT! IF YOU HADN'T ABANDONED HIM--
MY FAULT? LOOK, I'M NOT HERE TO PLAY BLOODY SIDEKICK. I JUST FIND THE NASTIES. TRASHING THEM IS ANGEL'S GIG.
HE'S A BIG BOY. HE CAN TAKE CARE OF HIMSELF.
STILL, HE SHOULDA BEEN BACK BY--
AAACHOO
OH, YEAH, ANGEL'S DONE SUCH A GREAT JOB TAKING CARE OF HIMSELF OVER THE YEARS. WHERE HAVE YOU BEEN?
AND, EEW, CAN I JUST SAY, KLEENEX?

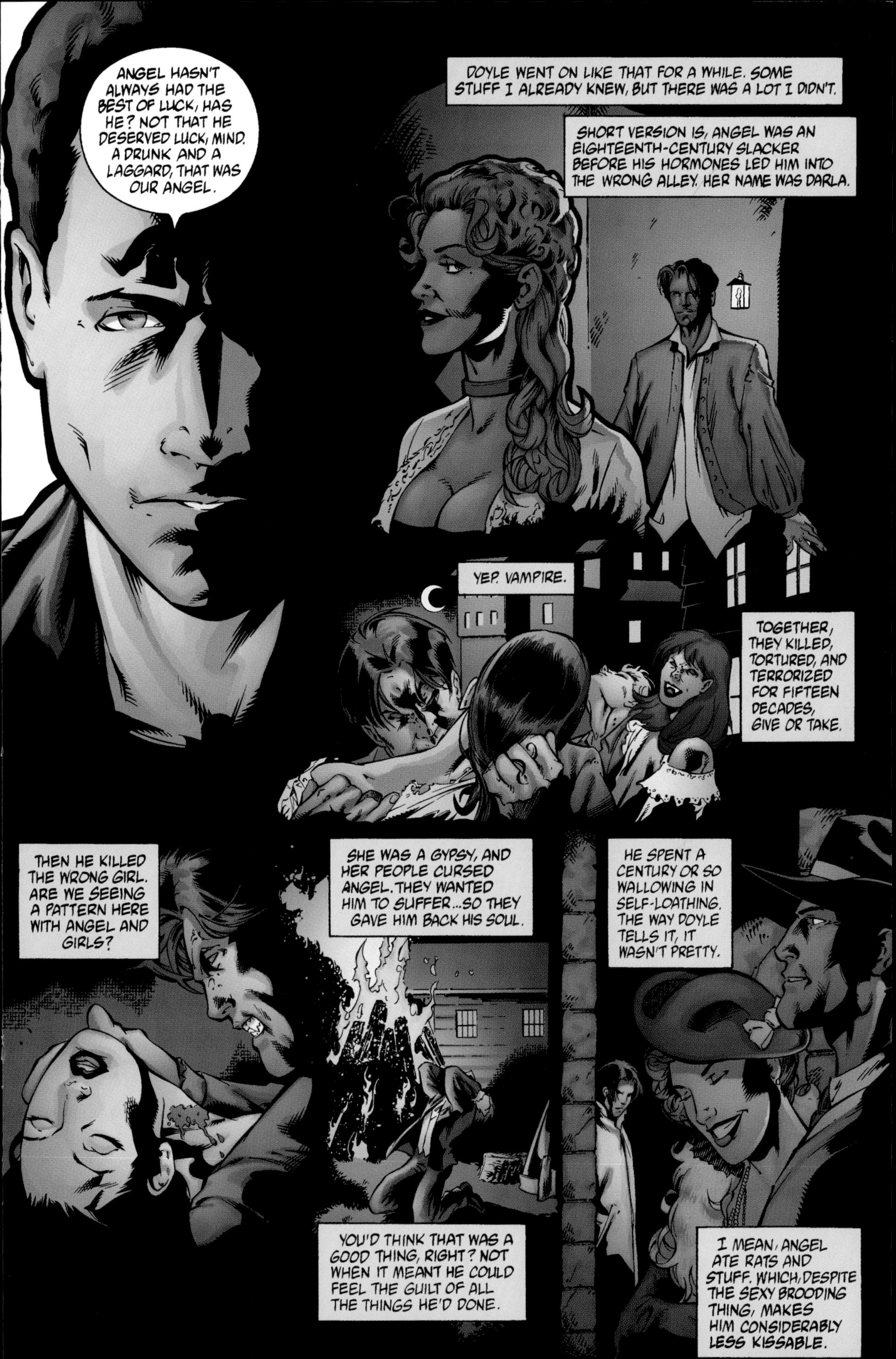
ANGEL HASN'T ALWAYS HAD THE BEST OF LUCK, HAS HE? NOT THAT HE DESERVED LUCK, MIND. A DRUNK AND A LAGGARD, THAT WAS OUR ANGEL.
DOYLE WENT ON LIKE THAT FOR A WHILE. SOME STUFF I ALREADY KNEW, BUT THERE WAS A LOT I DIDN'T.
SHORT VERSION IS, ANGEL WAS AN EIGHTEENTH-CENTURY SLACKER BEFORE HIS HORMONES LED HIM INTO THE WRONG ALLEY. HER NAME WAS DARLA.
YEP. VAMPIRE.
TOGETHER, THEY KILLED, TORTURED, AND TERRORIZED FOR FIFTEEN DECADES, GIVE OR TAKE.
THEN HE KILLED THE WRONG GIRL. ARE WE SEEING A PATTERN HERE WITH ANGEL AND GIRLS?
SHE WAS A GYPSY, AND HER PEOPLE CURSED ANGEL. THEY WANTED HIM TO SUFFER...SO THEY GAVE HIM BACK HIS SOUL.
YOU'D THINK THAT WAS A GOOD THING, RIGHT? NOT WHEN IT MEANT HE COULD FEEL THE GUILT OF ALL THE THINGS HE'D DONE.
HE SPENT A CENTURY OR SO WALLOWING IN SELF-LOATHING. THE WAY DOYLE TELLS IT, IT WASN'T PRETTY.
I MEAN, ANGEL ATE RATS AND STUFF. WHICH, DESPITE THE SEXY BROODING THING, MAKES HIM CONSIDERABLY LESS KISSABLE.

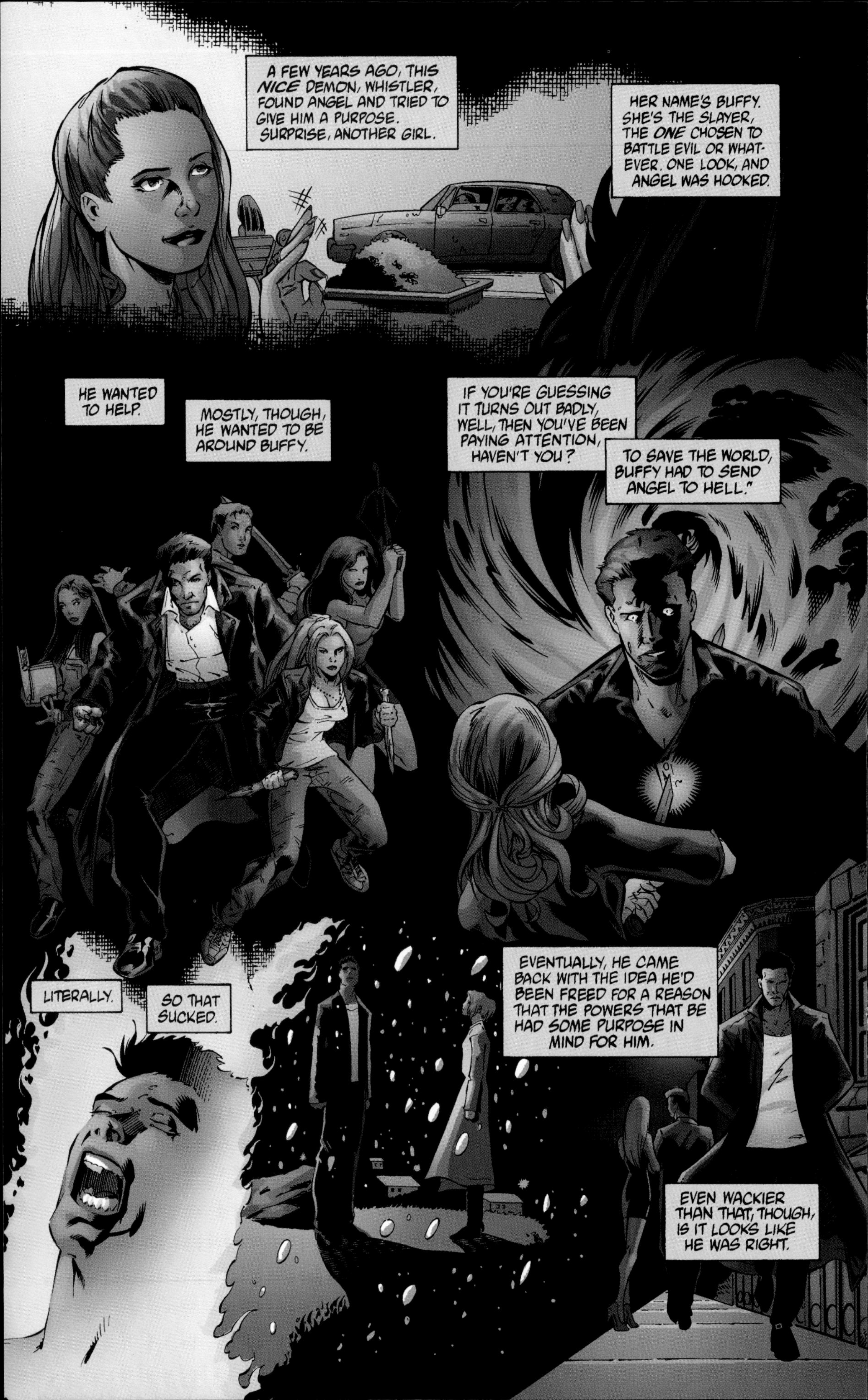
A FEW YEARS AGO, THIS NICE DEMON, WHISTLER, FOUND ANGEL AND TRIED TO GIVE HIM A PURPOSE. SURPRISE, ANOTHER GIRL.
HER NAME'S BUFFY. SHE'S THE SLAYER, THE ONE CHOSEN TO BATTLE EVIL OR WHATEVER. ONE LOOK, AND ANGEL WAS HOOKED.
HE WANTED TO HELP.
MOSTLY, THOUGH, HE WANTED TO BE AROUND BUFFY.
IF YOU'RE GUESSING IT TURNS OUT BADLY, WELL, THEN YOU'VE BEEN PAYING ATTENTION, HAVEN'T YOU?
TO SAVE THE WORLD, BUFFY HAD TO SEND ANGEL TO HELL."
LITERALLY.
SO THAT SUCKED.
EVENTUALLY, HE CAME BACK WITH THE IDEA HE'D BEEN FREED FOR A REASON THAT THE POWERS THAT BE HAD SOME PURPOSE IN MIND FOR HIM.
EVEN WACKIER THAN THAT, THOUGH, IS IT LOOKS LIKE HE WAS RIGHT.

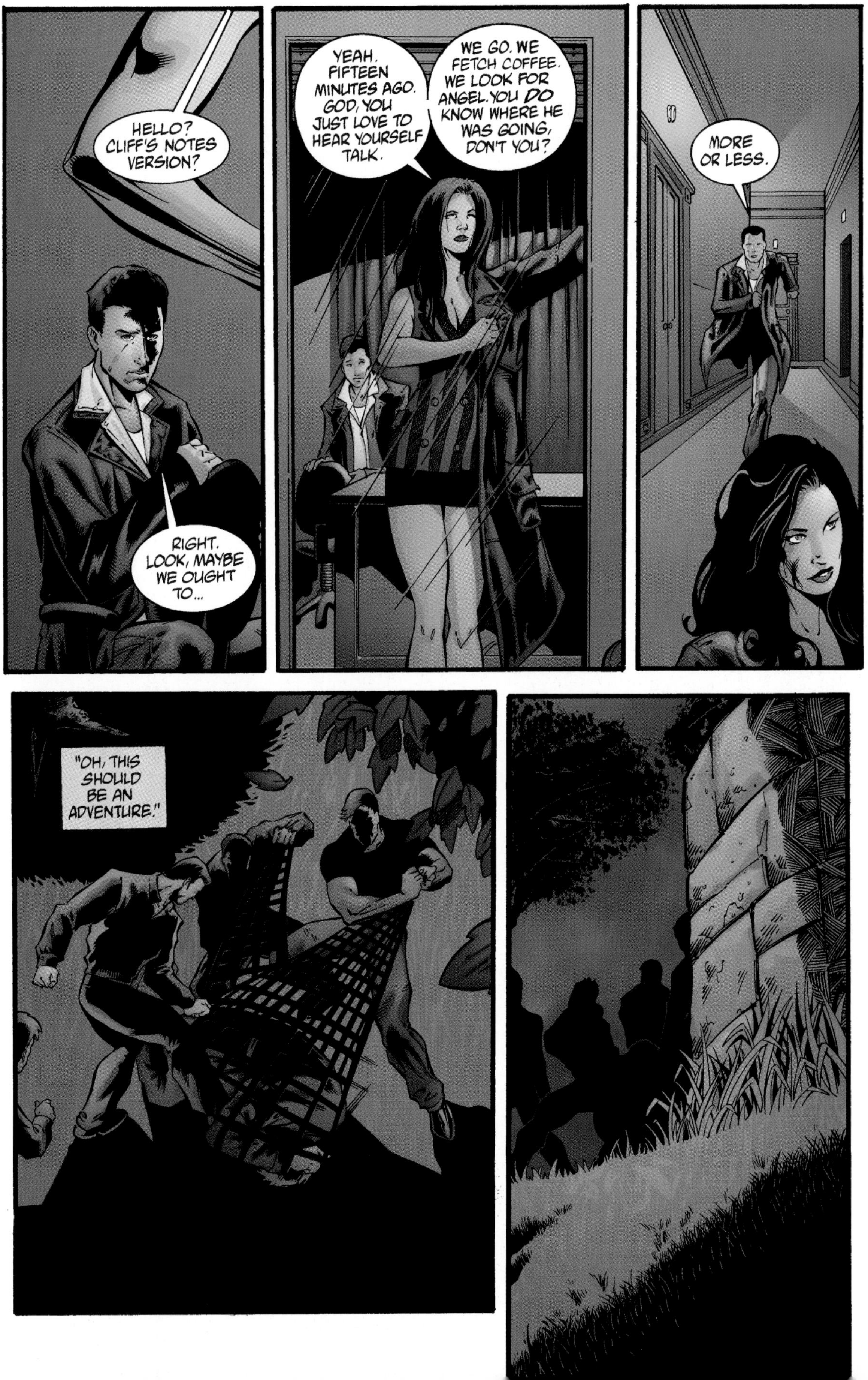
HELLO? CLIFF'S NOTES VERSION?
RIGHT. LOOK, MAYBE WE OUGHT TO...
YEAH. FIFTEEN MINUTES AGO. GOD, YOU JUST LOVE TO HEAR YOURSELF TALK.
WE GO. WE FETCH COFFEE. WE LOOK FOR ANGEL. YOU DO KNOW WHERE HE WAS GOING, DON'T YOU?
MORE OR LESS.
"OH, THIS SHOULD BE AN ADVENTURE."

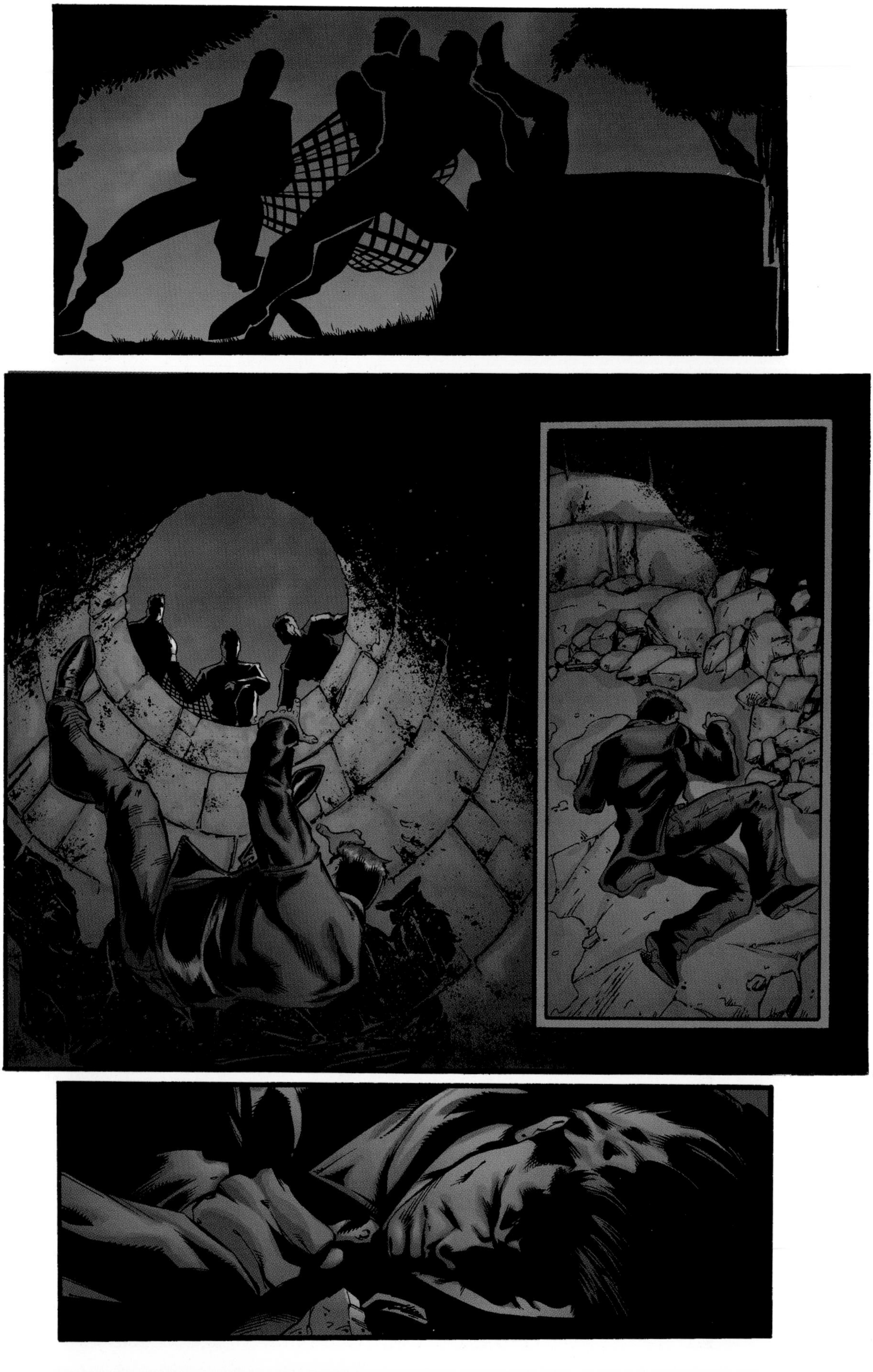

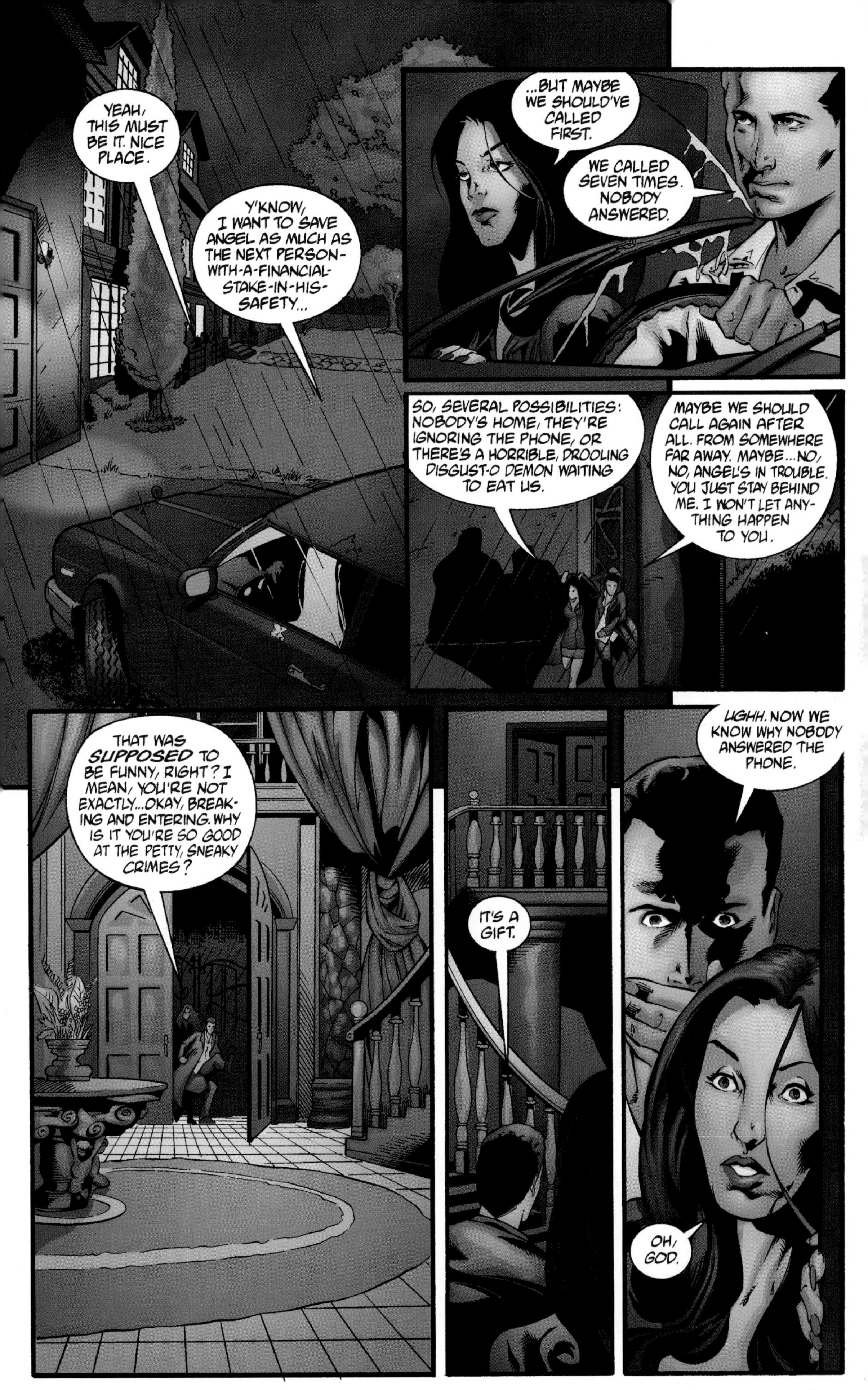
YEAH, THIS MUST BE IT. NICE PLACE.
Y'KNOW, I WANT TO SAVE ANGEL AS MUCH AS THE NEXT PERSON-WITH-A-FINANCIAL-STAKE-IN-HIS-SAFETY...
...BUT MAYBE WE SHOULD'VE CALLED FIRST.
WE CALLED SEVEN TIMES. NOBODY ANSWERED.
SO, SEVERAL POSSIBILITIES: NOBODY'S HOME, THEY'RE IGNORING THE PHONE, OR THERE'S A HORRIBLE, DROOLING DISGUST-O DEMON WAITING TO EAT US.
MAYBE WE SHOULD CALL AGAIN AFTER ALL. FROM SOMEWHERE FAR AWAY. MAYBE...NO, NO, ANGEL'S IN TROUBLE. YOU JUST STAY BEHIND ME. I WON'T LET ANYTHING HAPPEN TO YOU.
THAT WAS SUPPOSED TO BE FUNNY, RIGHT? I MEAN, YOU'RE NOT EXACTLY...OKAY, BREAKING AND ENTERING. WHY IS IT YOU'RE SO GOOD AT THE PETTY, SNEAKY CRIMES?
IT'S A GIFT.
UGHH. NOW WE KNOW WHY NOBODY ANSWERED THE PHONE.
OH, GOD.

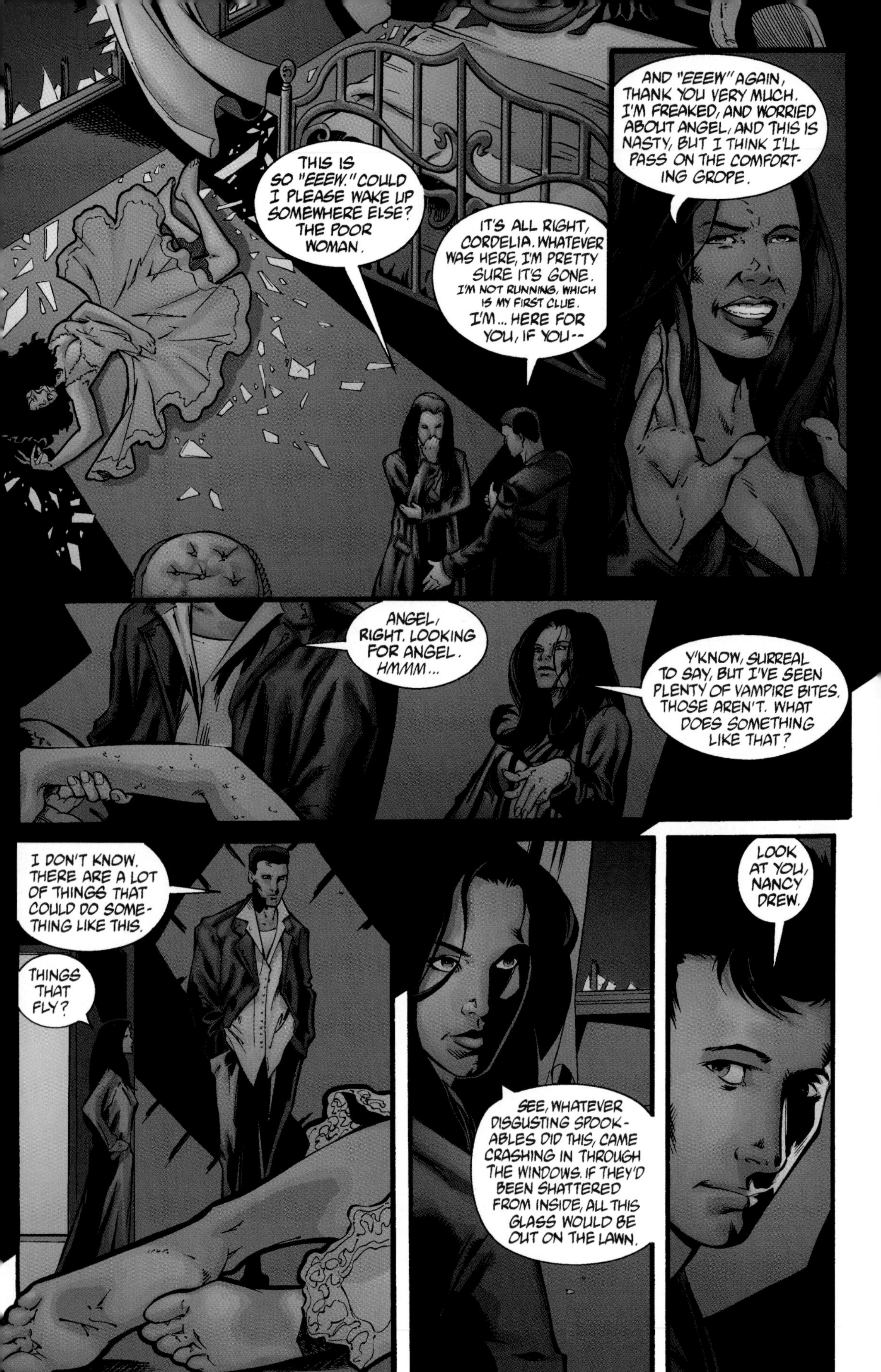
THIS IS SO "EEEW." COULD I PLEASE WAKE UP SOMEWHERE ELSE? THE POOR WOMAN.
IT'S ALL RIGHT, CORDELIA. WHATEVER WAS HERE, I'M PRETTY SURE IT'S GONE. I'M NOT RUNNING, WHICH IS MY FIRST CLUE. I'M... HERE FOR YOU, IF YOU--
AND "EEEW" AGAIN, THANK YOU VERY MUCH. I'M FREAKED, AND WORRIED ABOUT ANGEL, AND THIS IS NASTY, BUT I THINK I'LL PASS ON THE COMFORTING GROPE.
ANGEL, RIGHT. LOOKING FOR ANGEL. HMMM...
Y'KNOW, SURREAL TO SAY, BUT I'VE SEEN PLENTY OF VAMPIRE BITES. THOSE AREN'T. WHAT DOES SOMETHING LIKE THAT?
I DON'T KNOW. THERE ARE A LOT OF THINGS THAT COULD DO SOMETHING LIKE THIS.
THINGS THAT FLY?
SEE, WHATEVER DISGUSTING SPOOKABLES DID THIS, CAME CRASHING IN THROUGH THE WINDOWS. IF THEY'D BEEN SHATTERED FROM INSIDE, ALL THIS GLASS WOULD BE OUT ON THE LAWN.
LOOK AT YOU, NANCY DREW.

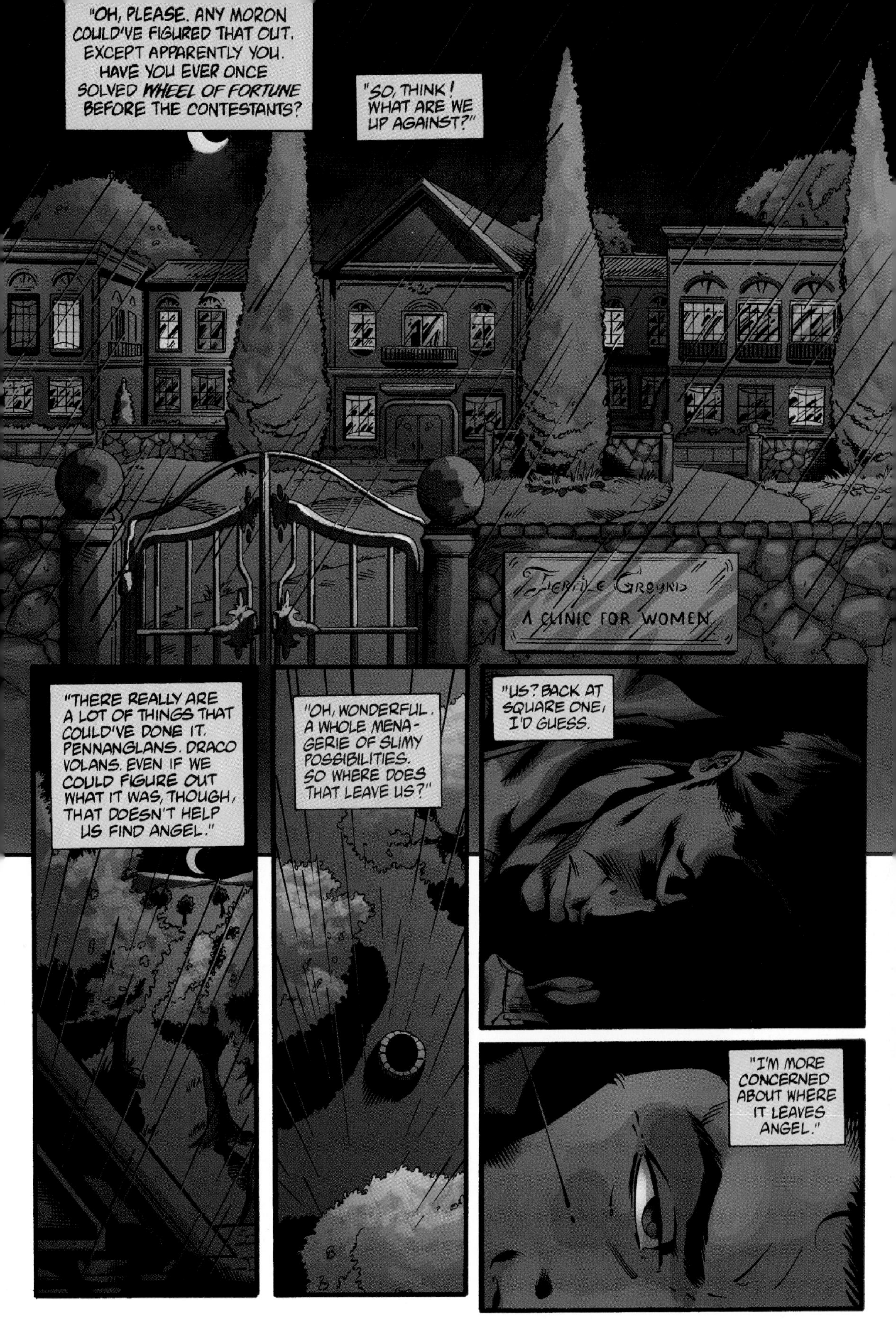
"OH, PLEASE. ANY MORON COULD'VE FIGURED THAT OUT. EXCEPT APPARENTLY YOU. HAVE YOU EVER ONCE SOLVED *WHEEL OF FORTUNE* BEFORE THE CONTESTANTS?
"SO, THINK! WHAT ARE WE UP AGAINST?"
FERTILE GROUND
A CLINIC FOR WOMEN
"THERE REALLY ARE A LOT OF THINGS THAT COULD'VE DONE IT. PENNANGLANS. DRACO VOLANS. EVEN IF WE COULD FIGURE OUT WHAT IT WAS, THOUGH, THAT DOESN'T HELP US FIND ANGEL."
"OH, WONDERFUL. A WHOLE MENAGERIE OF SLIMY POSSIBILITIES. SO WHERE DOES THAT LEAVE US?"
"US? BACK AT SQUARE ONE, I'D GUESS.
"I'M MORE CONCERNED ABOUT WHERE IT LEAVES ANGEL."

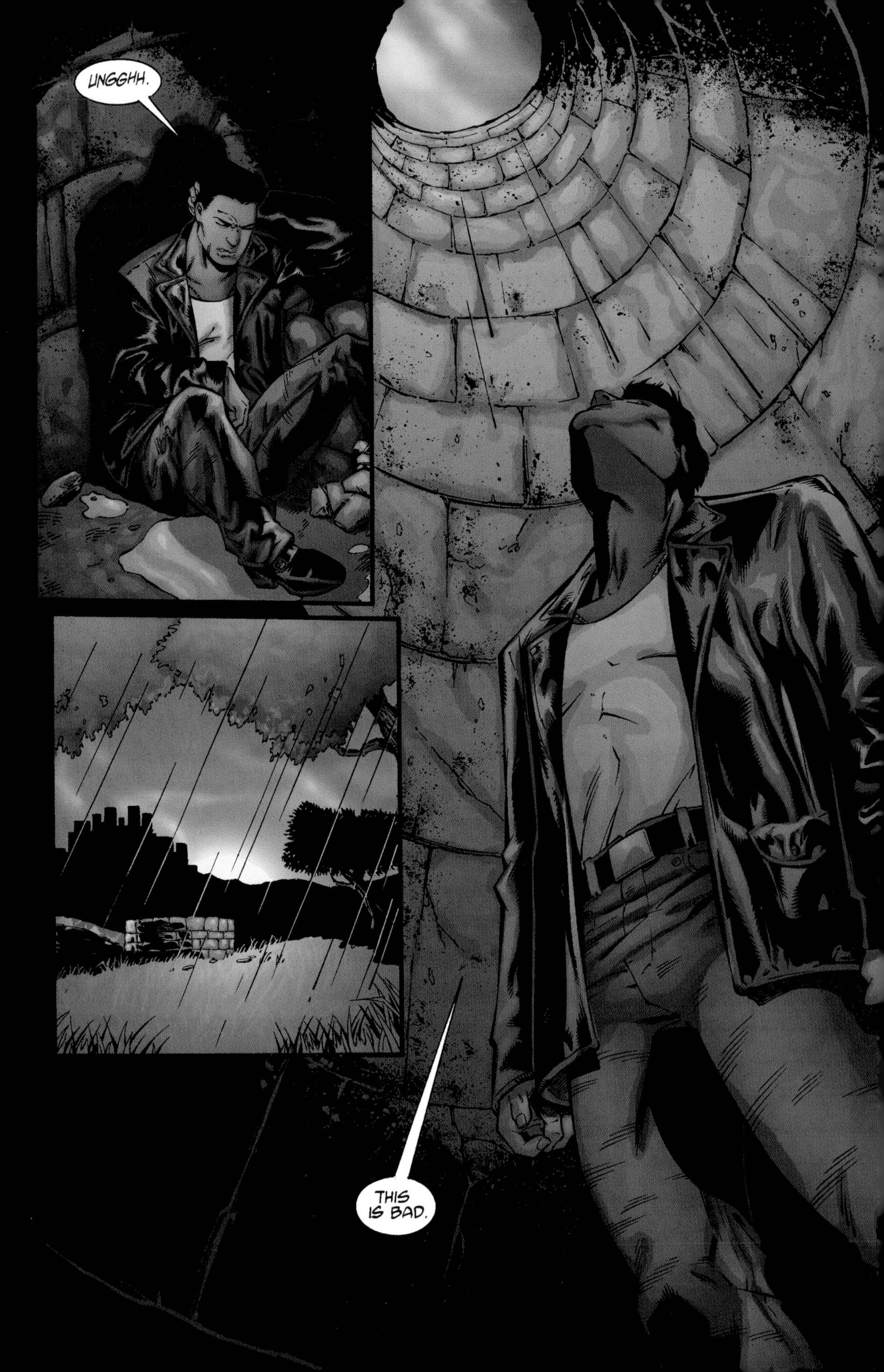
UNGGHH.
THIS IS BAD.

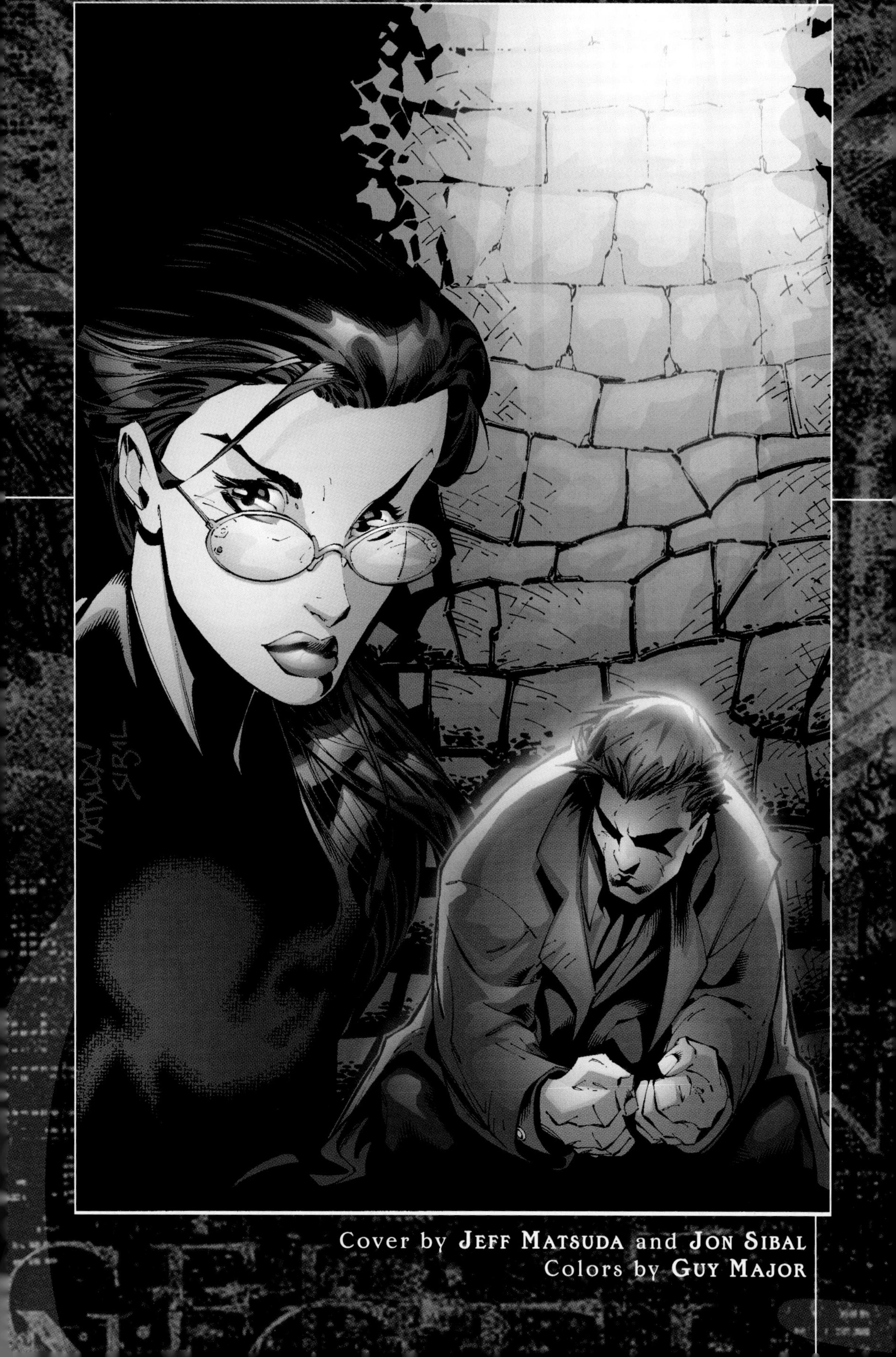

Cover by **Jeff Matsuda** and **Jon Sibal**
Colors by **Guy Major**

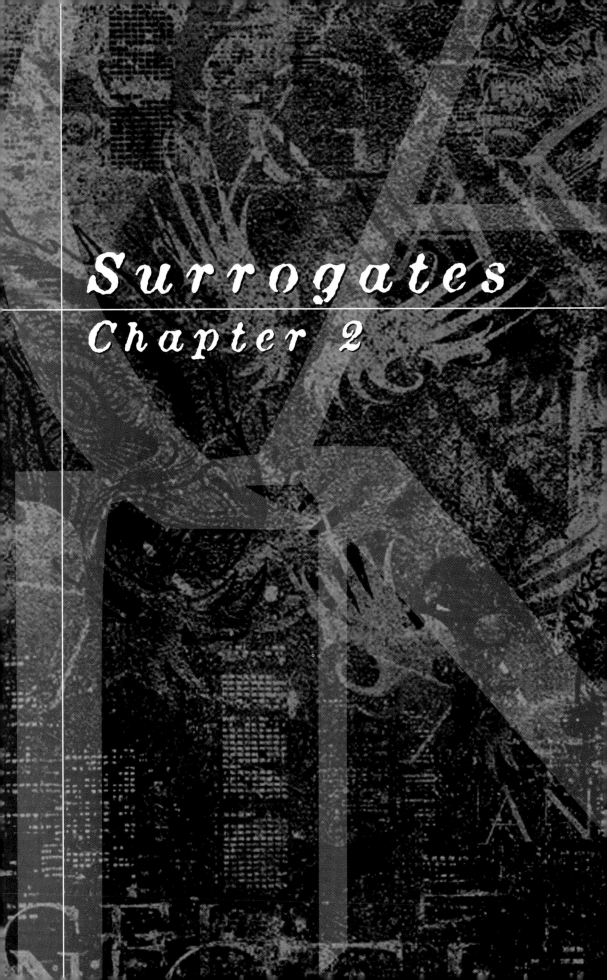

Surrogates
Chapter 2

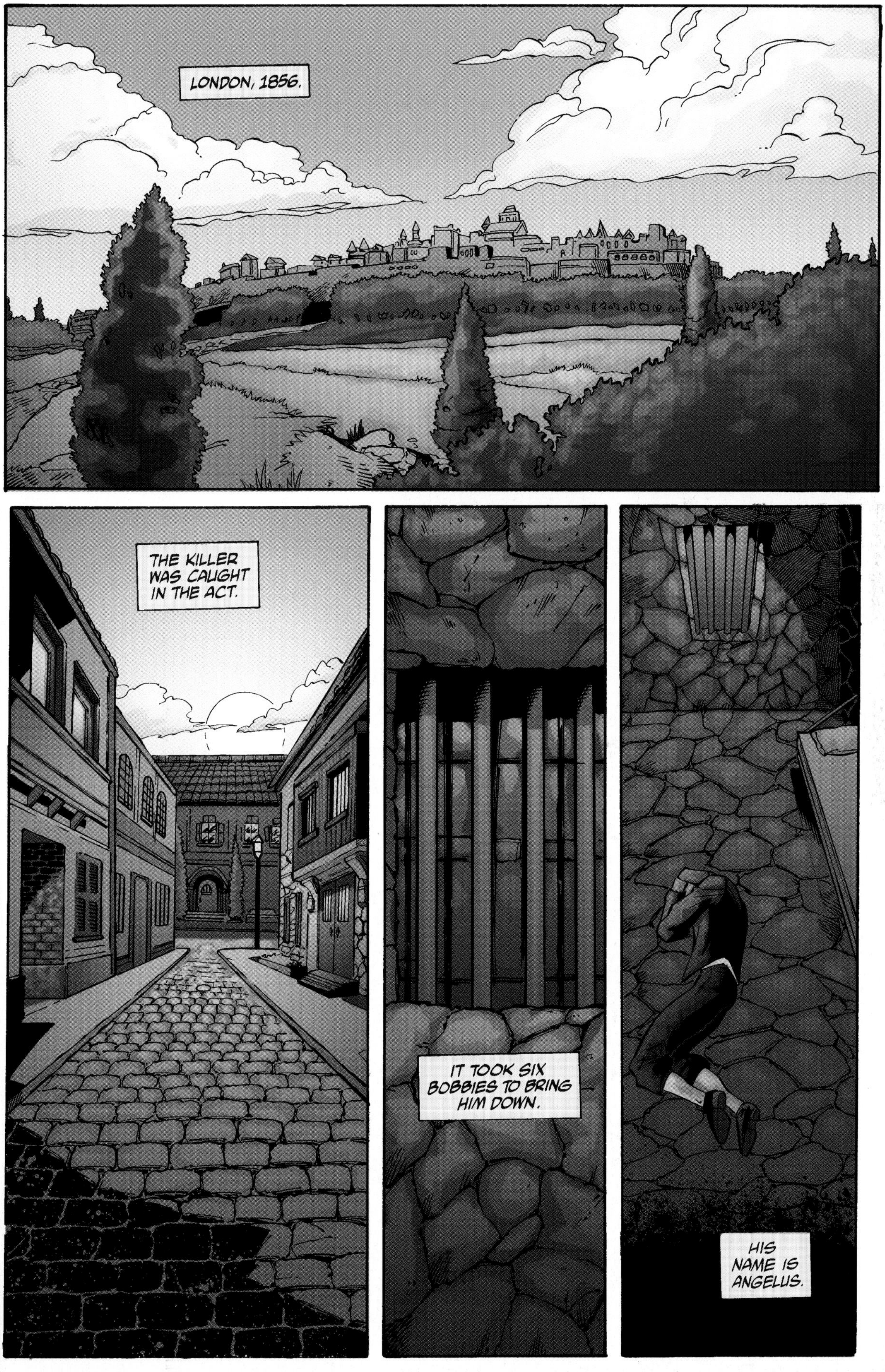
LONDON, 1856.
THE KILLER WAS CAUGHT IN THE ACT.
IT TOOK SIX BOBBIES TO BRING HIM DOWN.
HIS NAME IS ANGELUS.

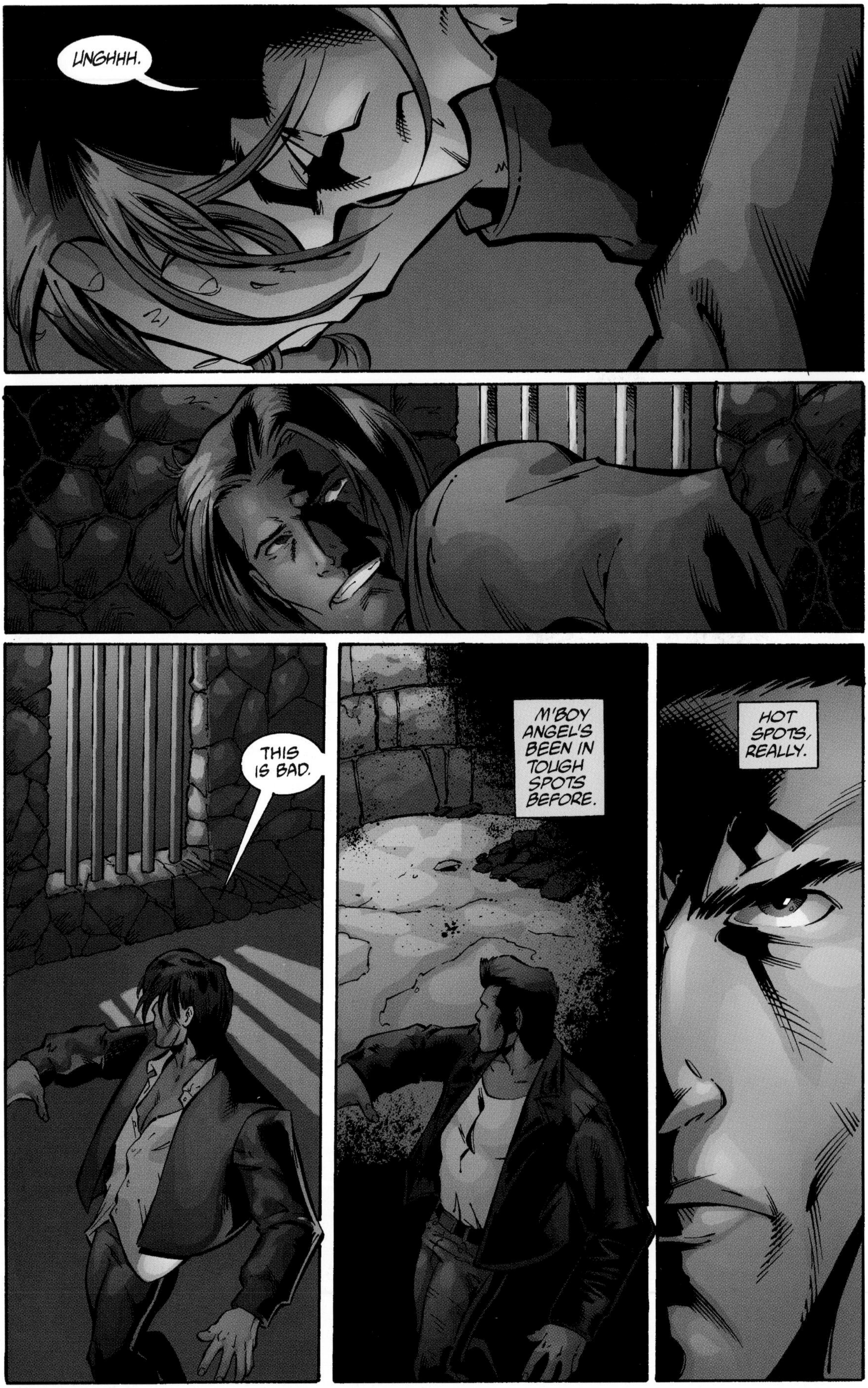
UNGHHH.
THIS IS BAD.
M'BOY ANGEL'S BEEN IN TOUGH SPOTS BEFORE.
HOT SPOTS, REALLY.

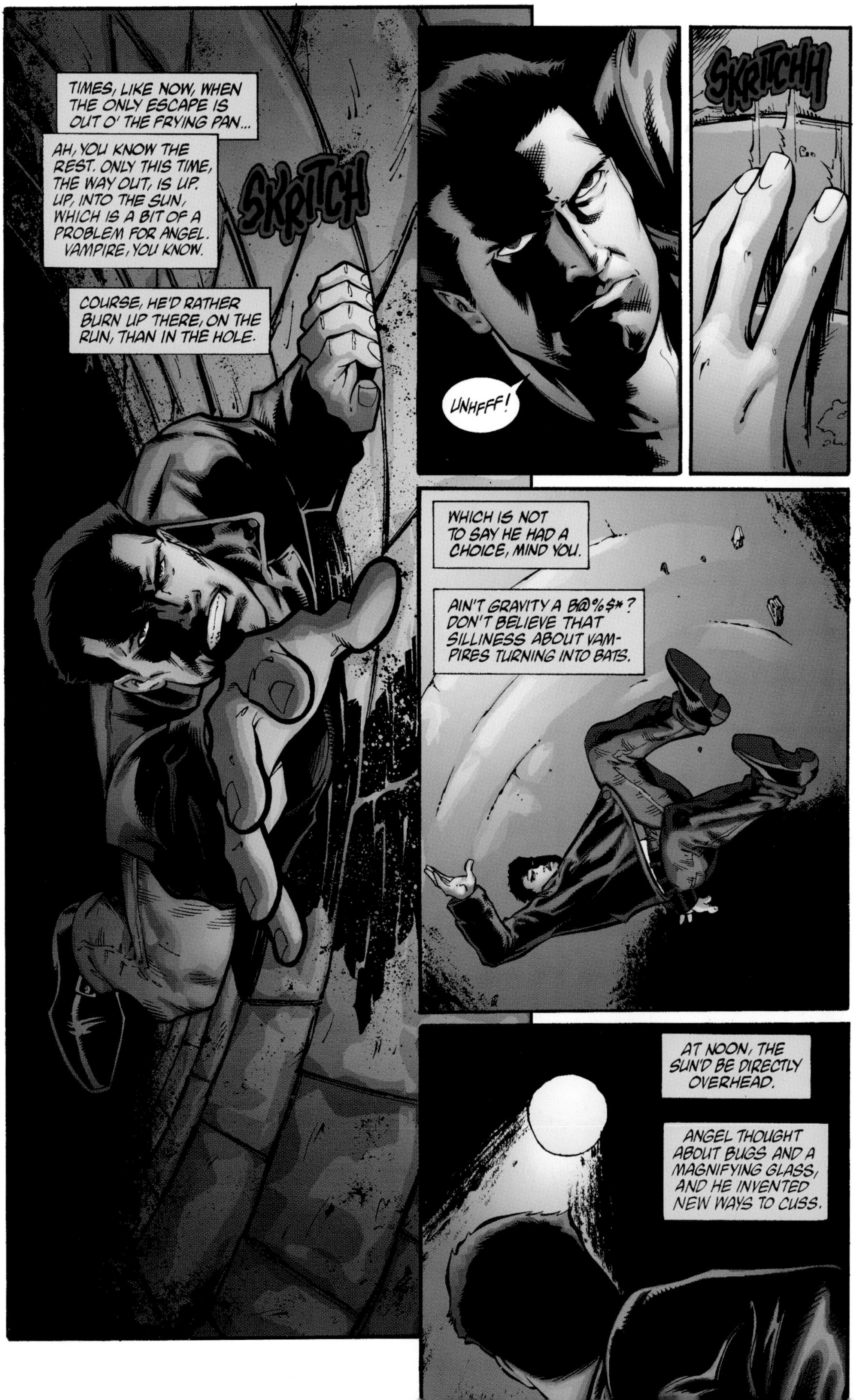
TIMES, LIKE NOW, WHEN THE ONLY ESCAPE IS OUT O' THE FRYING PAN...
AH, YOU KNOW THE REST. ONLY THIS TIME, THE WAY OUT, IS UP. UP, INTO THE SUN, WHICH IS A BIT OF A PROBLEM FOR ANGEL. VAMPIRE, YOU KNOW.
SKRITCH
COURSE, HE'D RATHER BURN UP THERE, ON THE RUN, THAN IN THE HOLE.
UNHFFF!
SKRITCHH
WHICH IS NOT TO SAY HE HAD A CHOICE, MIND YOU.
AIN'T GRAVITY A B@%$*? DON'T BELIEVE THAT SILLINESS ABOUT VAMPIRES TURNING INTO BATS.
AT NOON, THE SUN'D BE DIRECTLY OVERHEAD.
ANGEL THOUGHT ABOUT BUGS AND A MAGNIFYING GLASS, AND HE INVENTED NEW WAYS TO CUSS.

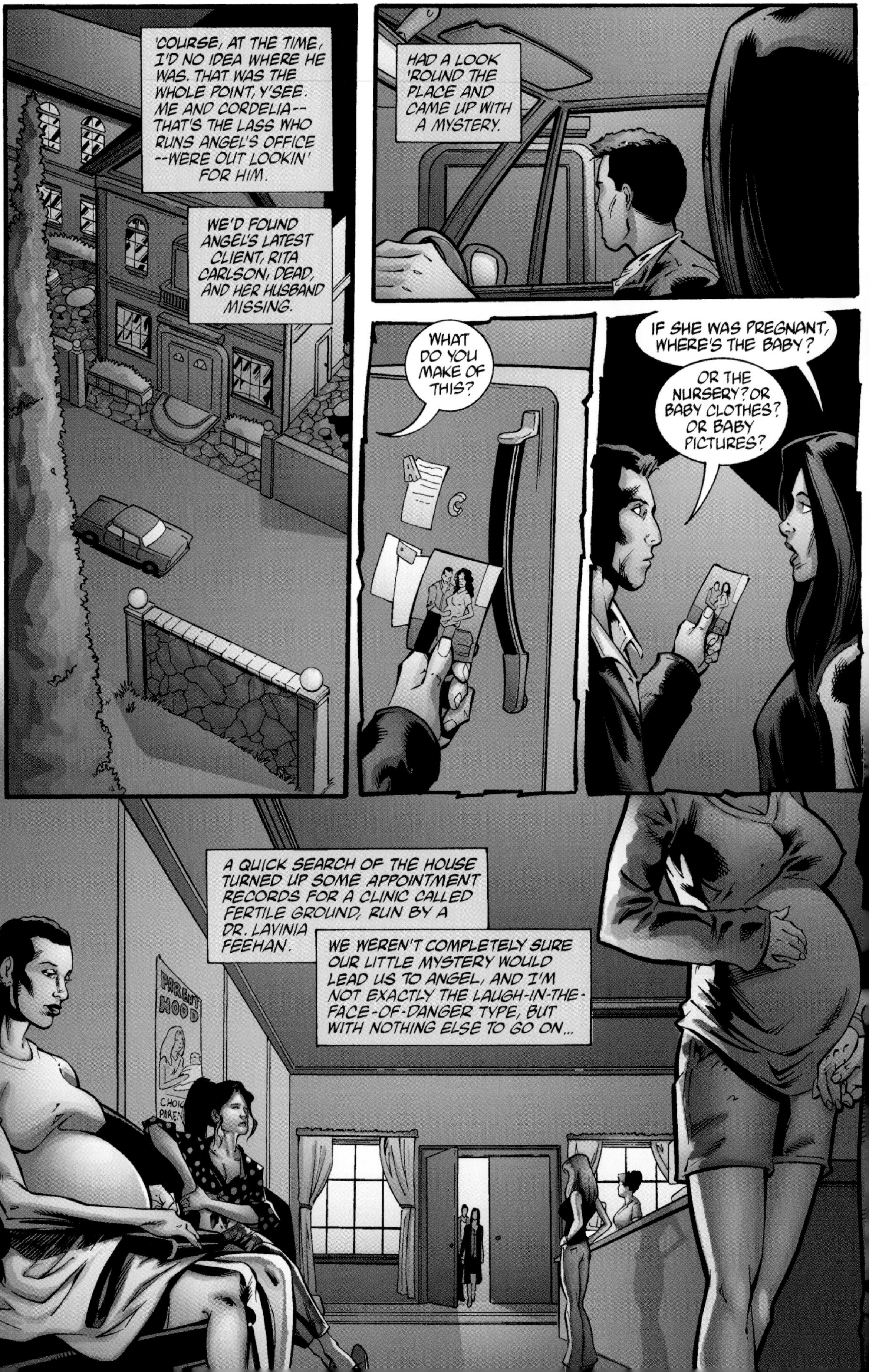
'COURSE, AT THE TIME, I'D NO IDEA WHERE HE WAS. THAT WAS THE WHOLE POINT, Y'SEE. ME AND CORDELIA-- THAT'S THE LASS WHO RUNS ANGEL'S OFFICE --WERE OUT LOOKIN' FOR HIM.
WE'D FOUND ANGEL'S LATEST CLIENT, RITA CARLSON, DEAD, AND HER HUSBAND MISSING.
HAD A LOOK 'ROUND THE PLACE AND CAME UP WITH A MYSTERY.
WHAT DO YOU MAKE OF THIS?
IF SHE WAS PREGNANT, WHERE'S THE BABY?
OR THE NURSERY? OR BABY CLOTHES? OR BABY PICTURES?
A QUICK SEARCH OF THE HOUSE TURNED UP SOME APPOINTMENT RECORDS FOR A CLINIC CALLED FERTILE GROUND, RUN BY A DR. LAVINIA FEEHAN.
WE WEREN'T COMPLETELY SURE OUR LITTLE MYSTERY WOULD LEAD US TO ANGEL, AND I'M NOT EXACTLY THE LAUGH-IN-THE-FACE-OF-DANGER TYPE, BUT WITH NOTHING ELSE TO GO ON...

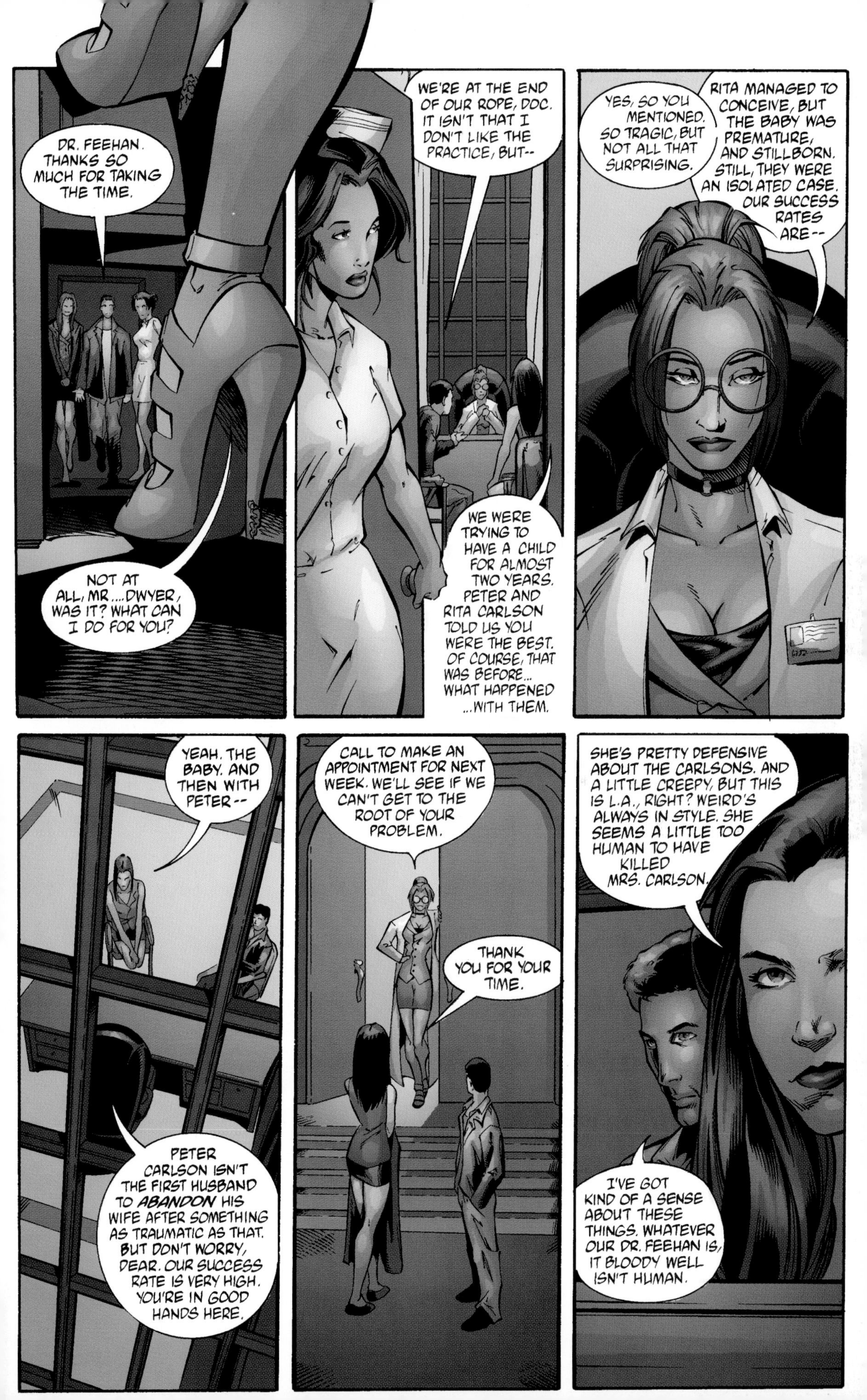
DR. FEEHAN. THANKS SO MUCH FOR TAKING THE TIME.
NOT AT ALL, MR.... DWYER, WAS IT? WHAT CAN I DO FOR YOU?
WE'RE AT THE END OF OUR ROPE, DOC. IT ISN'T THAT I DON'T LIKE THE PRACTICE, BUT--
WE WERE TRYING TO HAVE A CHILD FOR ALMOST TWO YEARS. PETER AND RITA CARLSON TOLD US YOU WERE THE BEST. OF COURSE, THAT WAS BEFORE... WHAT HAPPENED ...WITH THEM.
YES, SO YOU MENTIONED. SO TRAGIC, BUT NOT ALL THAT SURPRISING.
RITA MANAGED TO CONCEIVE, BUT THE BABY WAS PREMATURE, AND STILLBORN. STILL, THEY WERE AN ISOLATED CASE. OUR SUCCESS RATES ARE--
YEAH. THE BABY. AND THEN WITH PETER--
PETER CARLSON ISN'T THE FIRST HUSBAND TO *ABANDON* HIS WIFE AFTER SOMETHING AS TRAUMATIC AS THAT. BUT DON'T WORRY, DEAR. OUR SUCCESS RATE IS VERY HIGH. YOU'RE IN GOOD HANDS HERE.
CALL TO MAKE AN APPOINTMENT FOR NEXT WEEK. WE'LL SEE IF WE CAN'T GET TO THE ROOT OF YOUR PROBLEM.
THANK YOU FOR YOUR TIME.
SHE'S PRETTY DEFENSIVE ABOUT THE CARLSONS. AND A LITTLE CREEPY, BUT THIS IS L.A., RIGHT? WEIRD'S ALWAYS IN STYLE. SHE SEEMS A LITTLE TOO HUMAN TO HAVE KILLED MRS. CARLSON.
I'VE GOT KIND OF A SENSE ABOUT THESE THINGS. WHATEVER OUR DR. FEEHAN IS, IT BLOODY WELL ISN'T HUMAN.

SO WE KNEW WE WERE ONTO SOMETHING.

WE KNEW WHERE TO START LOOKING FOR ANGEL. THE CLOCK WAS TICKING.

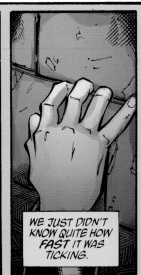

WE JUST DIDN'T KNOW QUITE HOW FAST IT WAS TICKING.

GRARRRHH!

ONLY THING WE WERE PRETTY SURE OF WAS THAT ANGEL'D BEEN THERE BEFORE US. AND SINCE HE HADN'T COME BACK, WELL... LOGIC SAID HE WAS PROBABLY STILL THERE.

FERTILE
A CLINIC FOR

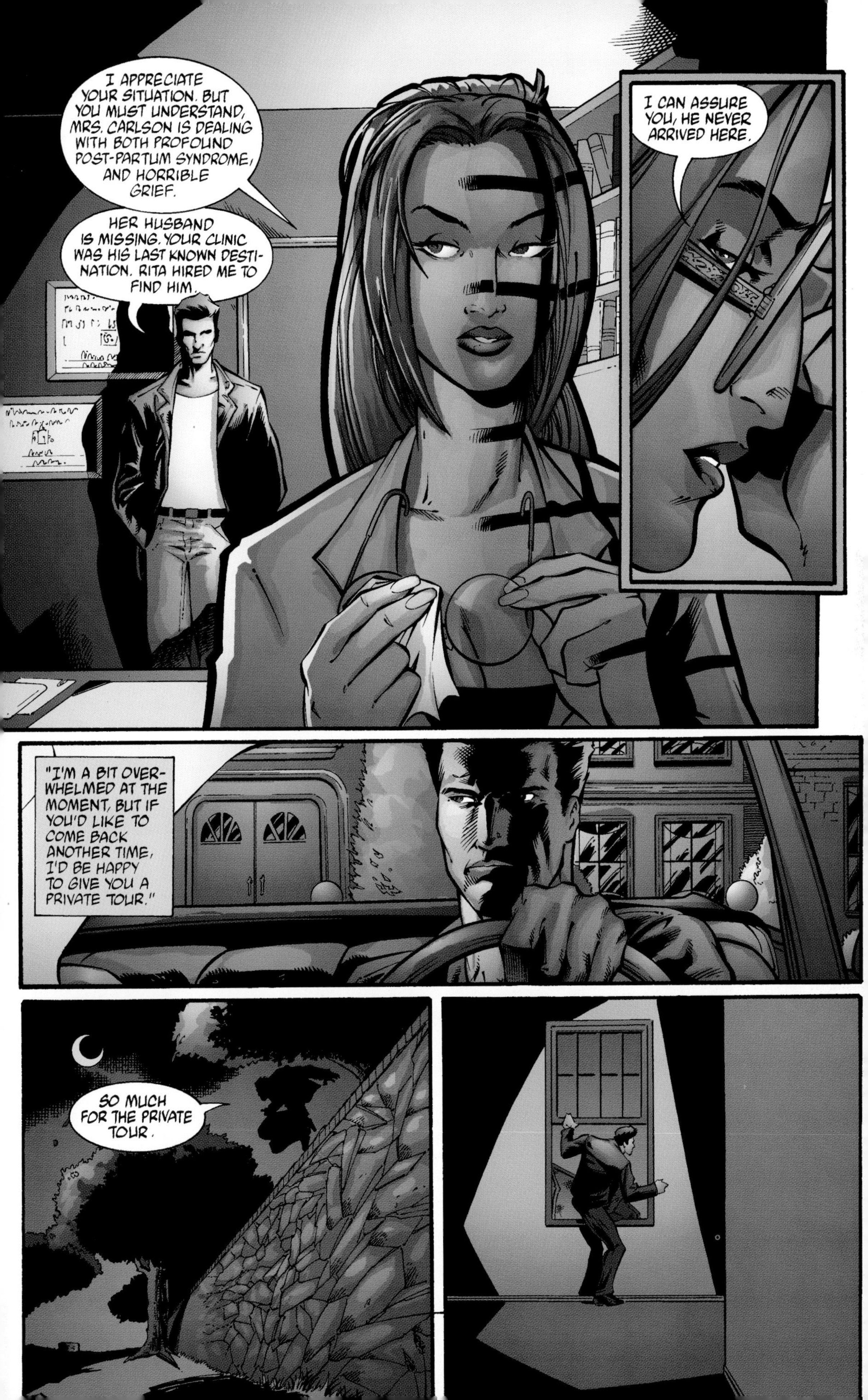
I APPRECIATE YOUR SITUATION. BUT YOU MUST UNDERSTAND, MRS. CARLSON IS DEALING WITH BOTH PROFOUND POST-PARTUM SYNDROME, AND HORRIBLE GRIEF.
HER HUSBAND IS MISSING. YOUR CLINIC WAS HIS LAST KNOWN DESTINATION. RITA HIRED ME TO FIND HIM.
I CAN ASSURE YOU, HE NEVER ARRIVED HERE.
"I'M A BIT OVERWHELMED AT THE MOMENT, BUT IF YOU'D LIKE TO COME BACK ANOTHER TIME, I'D BE HAPPY TO GIVE YOU A PRIVATE TOUR."
SO MUCH FOR THE PRIVATE TOUR.

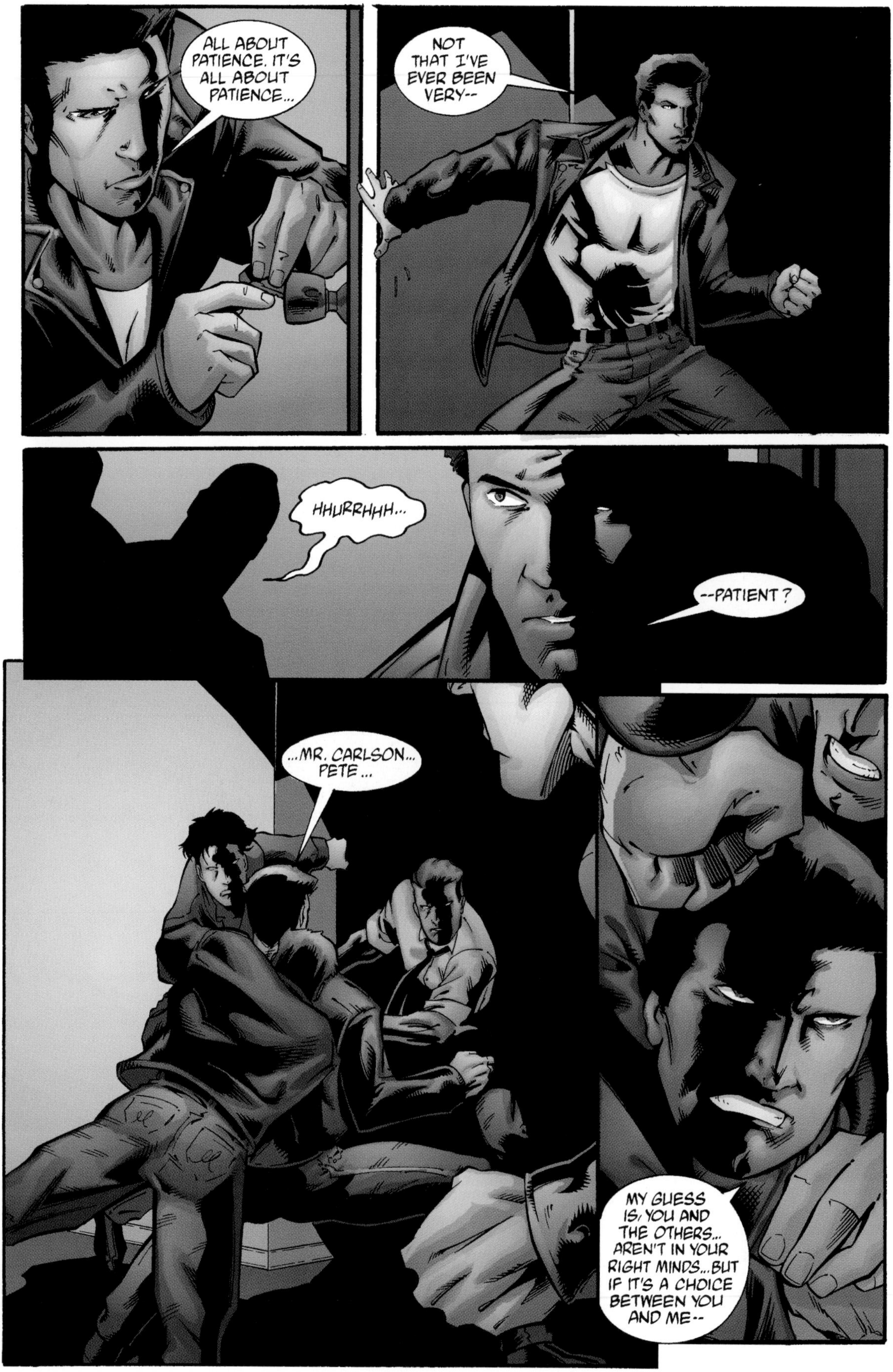
ALL ABOUT PATIENCE. IT'S ALL ABOUT PATIENCE...
NOT THAT I'VE EVER BEEN VERY--
HHURRHHH...
--PATIENT?
...MR. CARLSON... PETE ...
MY GUESS IS, YOU AND THE OTHERS... AREN'T IN YOUR RIGHT MINDS...BUT IF IT'S A CHOICE BETWEEN YOU AND ME--

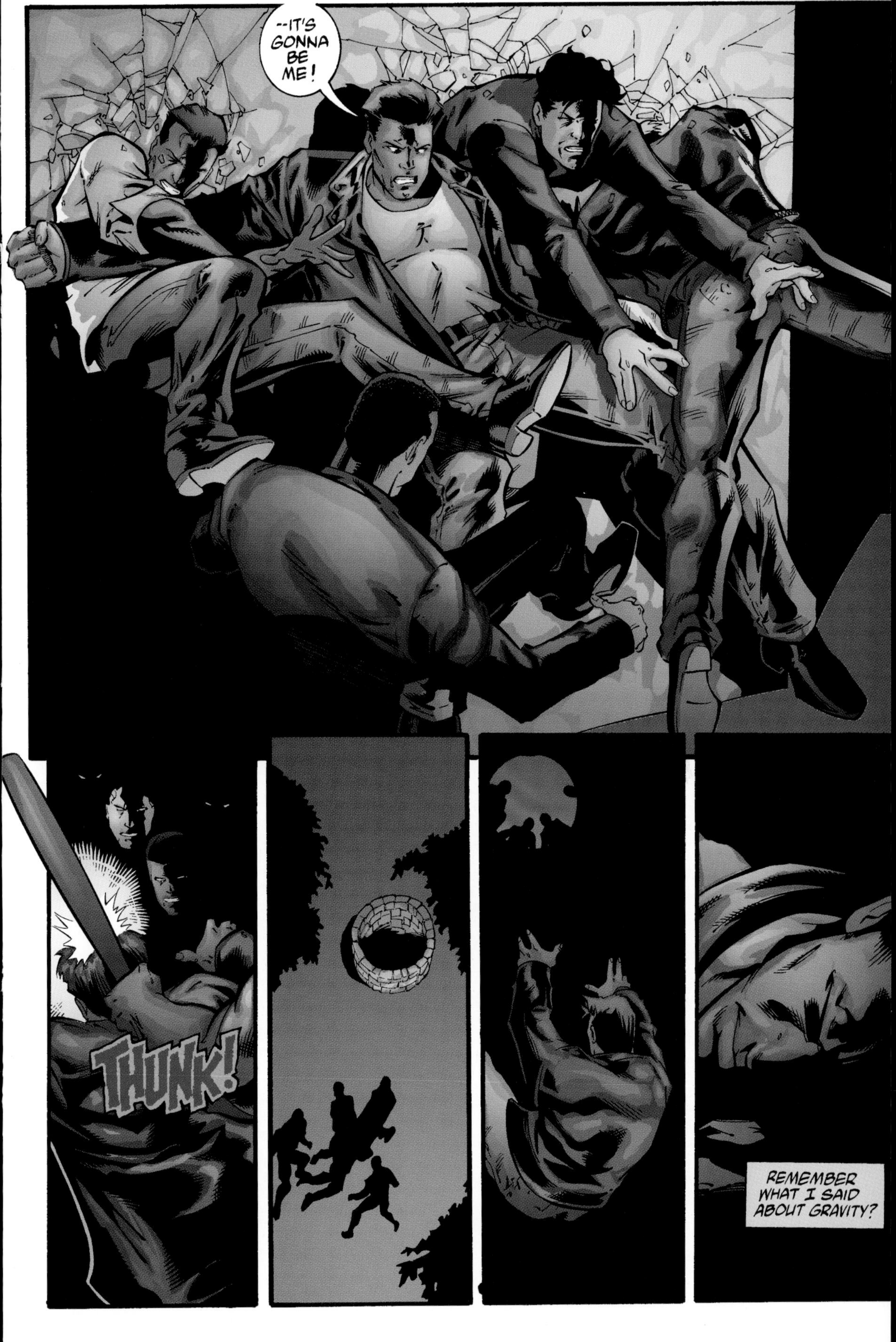
--IT'S GONNA BE ME!
THUNK!
REMEMBER WHAT I SAID ABOUT GRAVITY?

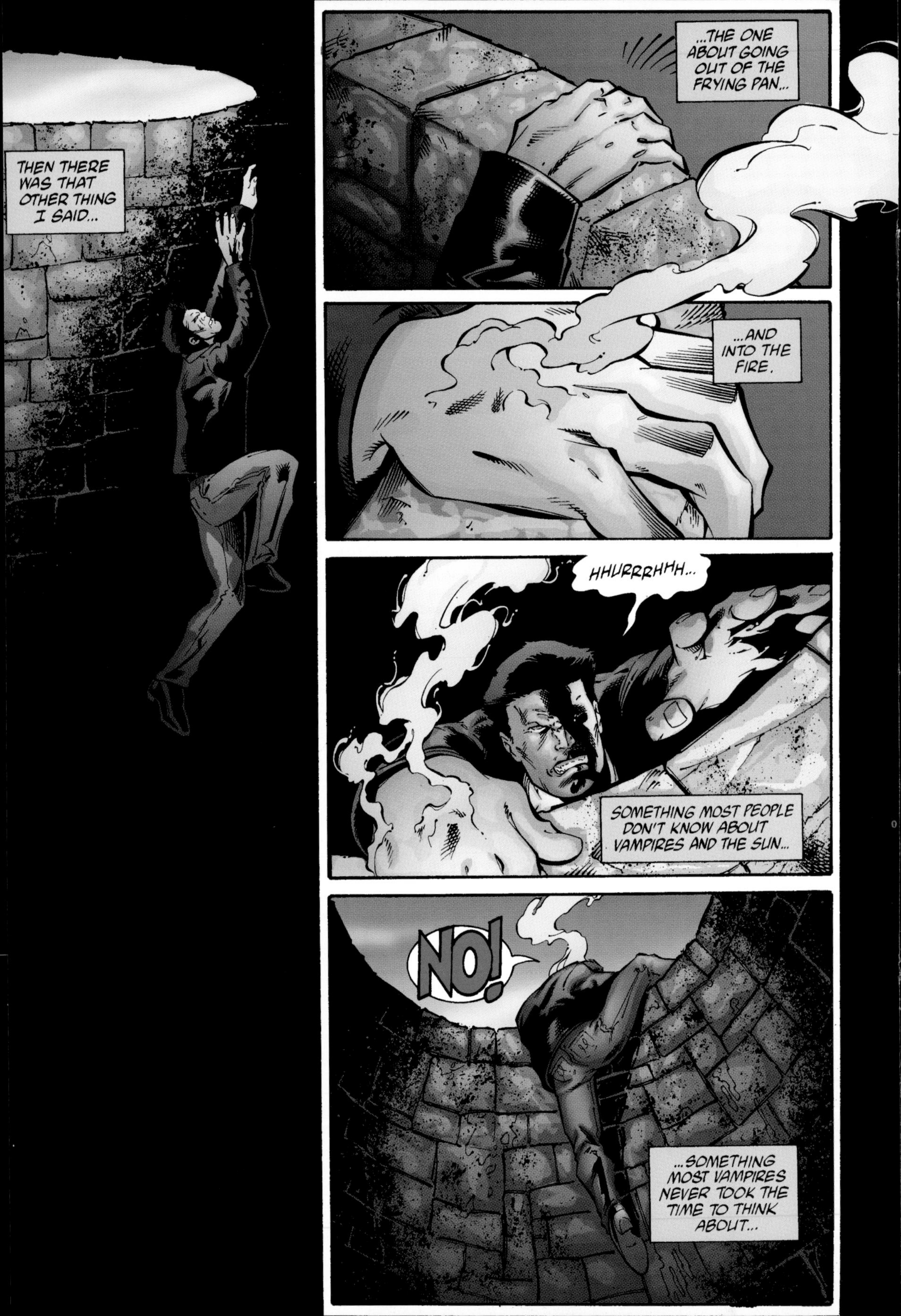
THEN THERE WAS THAT OTHER THING I SAID...
...THE ONE ABOUT GOING OUT OF THE FRYING PAN...
...AND INTO THE FIRE.
HHURRRHHH...
SOMETHING MOST PEOPLE DON'T KNOW ABOUT VAMPIRES AND THE SUN...
NO!
...SOMETHING MOST VAMPIRES NEVER TOOK THE TIME TO THINK ABOUT...

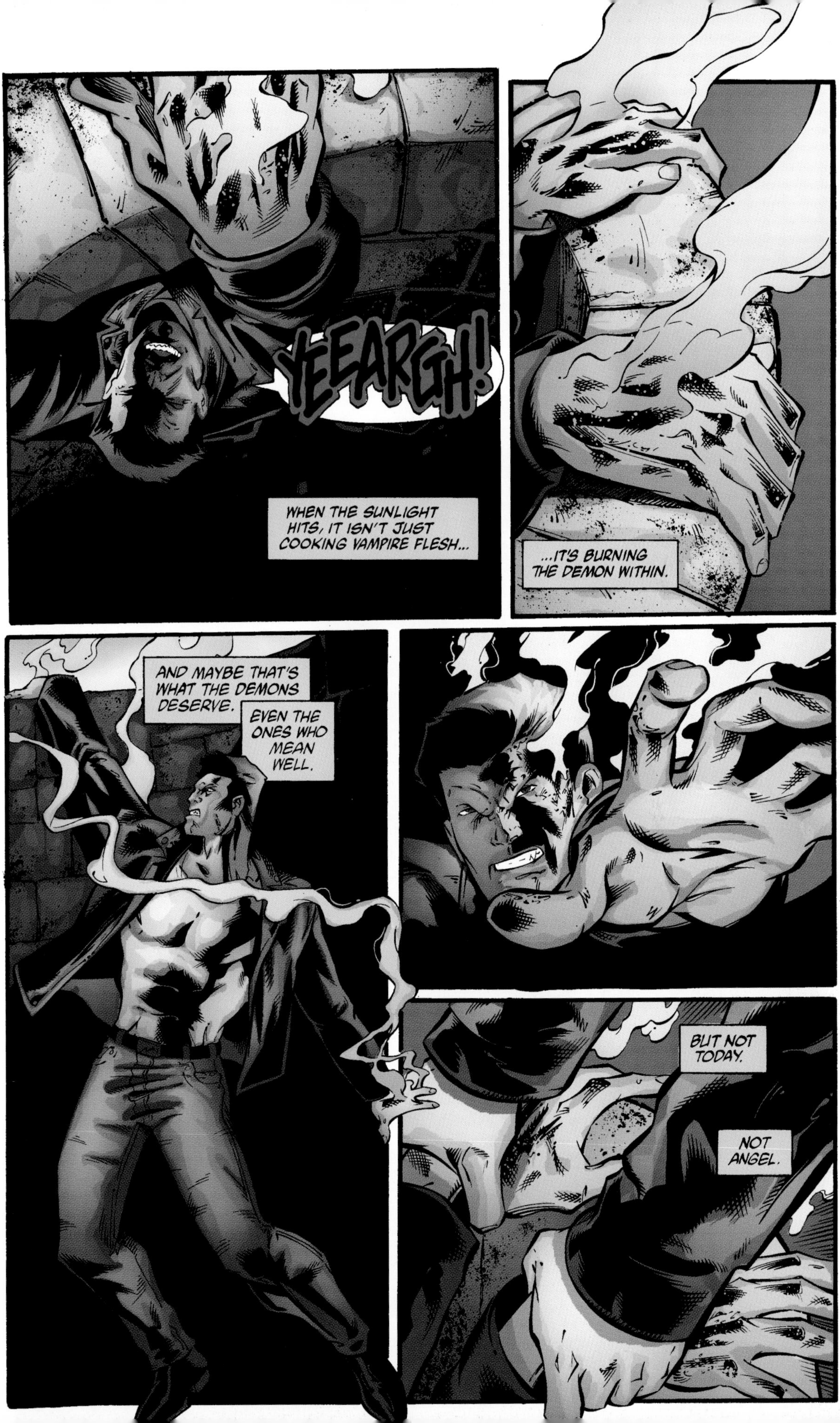
YEEARGH!
WHEN THE SUNLIGHT HITS, IT ISN'T JUST COOKING VAMPIRE FLESH...
...IT'S BURNING THE DEMON WITHIN.
AND MAYBE THAT'S WHAT THE DEMONS DESERVE.
EVEN THE ONES WHO MEAN WELL.
BUT NOT TODAY.
NOT ANGEL.

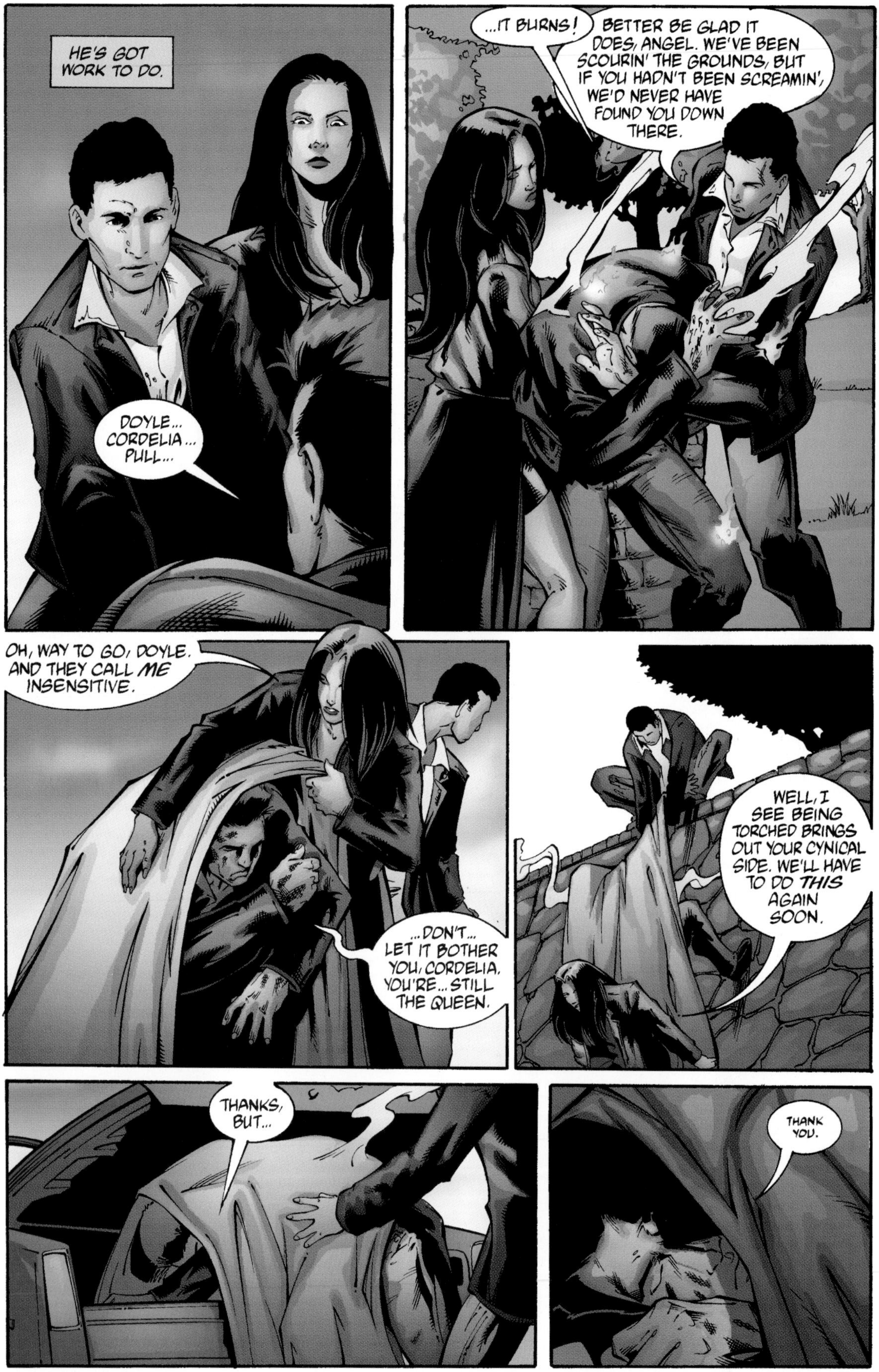
HE'S GOT WORK TO DO.
DOYLE... CORDELIA... PULL...
...IT BURNS!
BETTER BE GLAD IT DOES, ANGEL. WE'VE BEEN SCOURIN' THE GROUNDS, BUT IF YOU HADN'T BEEN SCREAMIN', WE'D NEVER HAVE FOUND YOU DOWN THERE.
OH, WAY TO GO, DOYLE. AND THEY CALL ME INSENSITIVE.
...DON'T... LET IT BOTHER YOU, CORDELIA. YOU'RE... STILL THE QUEEN.
WELL, I SEE BEING TORCHED BRINGS OUT YOUR CYNICAL SIDE. WE'LL HAVE TO DO THIS AGAIN SOON.
THANKS, BUT...
THANK YOU.

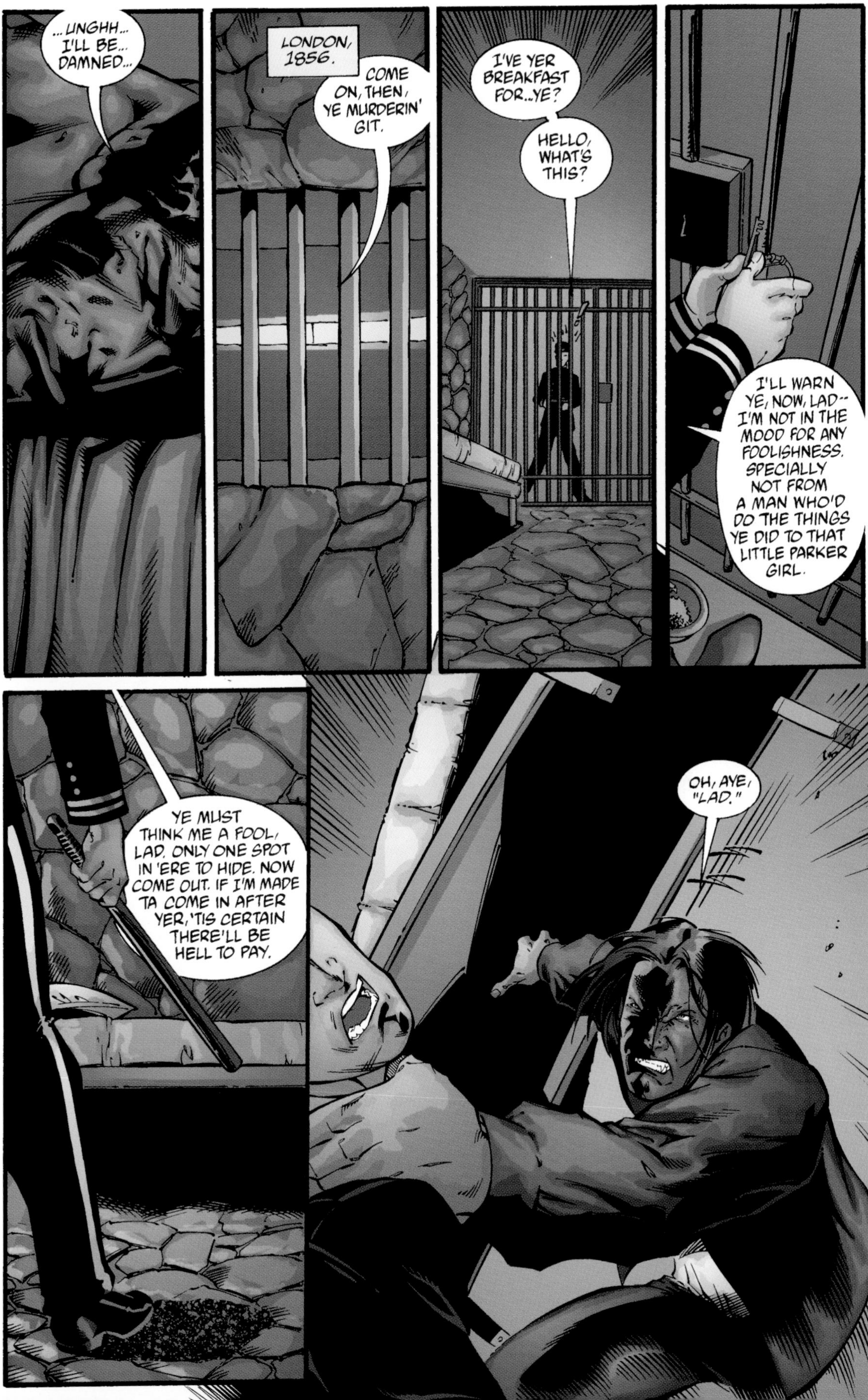
...UNGHH... I'LL BE... DAMNED...
LONDON, 1856.
COME ON, THEN, YE MURDERIN' GIT.
I'VE YER BREAKFAST FOR..YE?
HELLO, WHAT'S THIS?
I'LL WARN YE, NOW, LAD-- I'M NOT IN THE MOOD FOR ANY FOOLISHNESS. SPECIALLY NOT FROM A MAN WHO'D DO THE THINGS YE DID TO THAT LITTLE PARKER GIRL.
YE MUST THINK ME A FOOL, LAD. ONLY ONE SPOT IN 'ERE TO HIDE. NOW COME OUT. IF I'M MADE TA COME IN AFTER YER, 'TIS CERTAIN THERE'LL BE HELL TO PAY.
OH, AYE, "LAD."

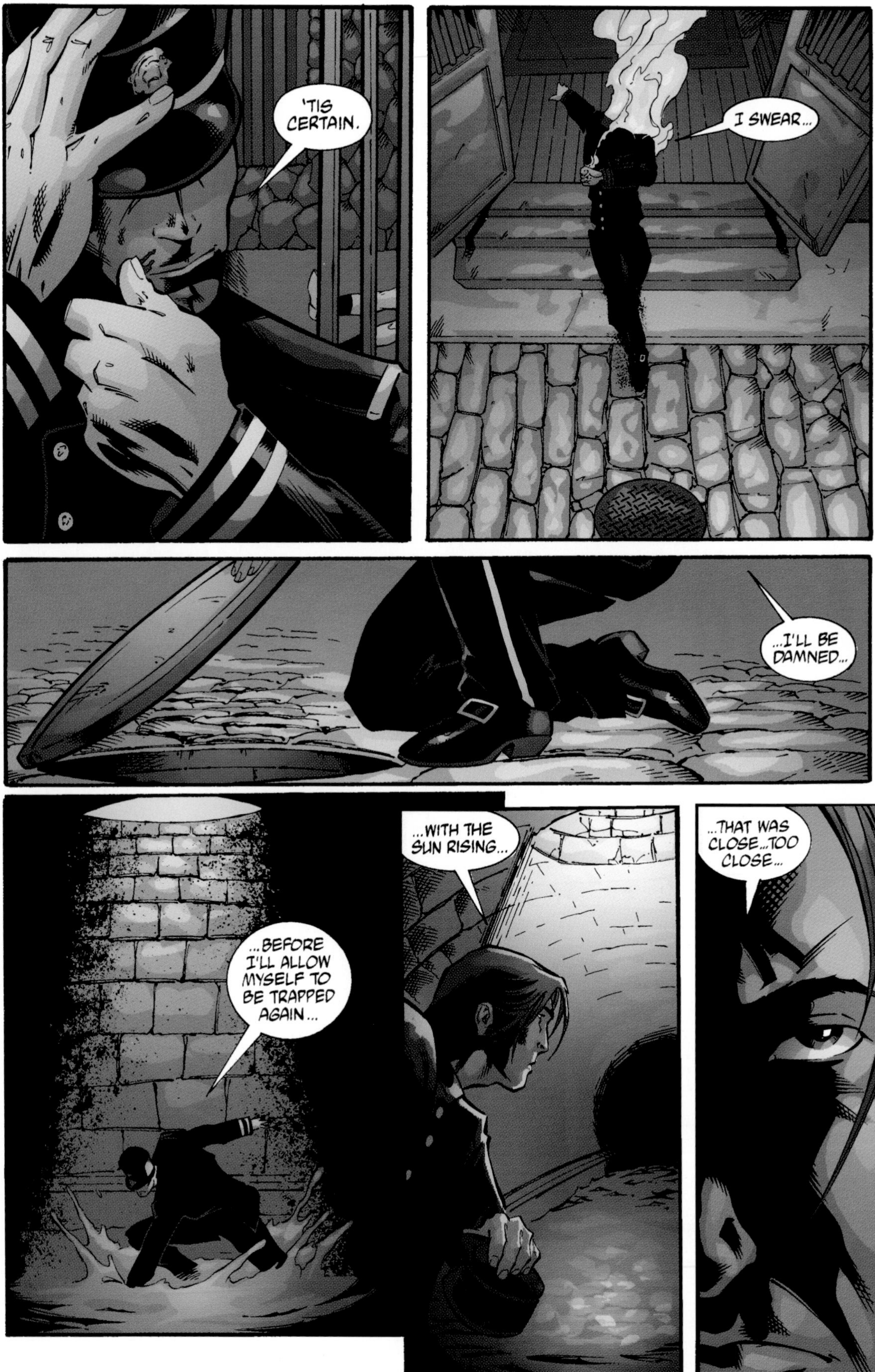
'TIS CERTAIN.
I SWEAR...
...I'LL BE DAMNED...
...BEFORE I'LL ALLOW MYSELF TO BE TRAPPED AGAIN...
...WITH THE SUN RISING...
...THAT WAS CLOSE...TOO CLOSE...

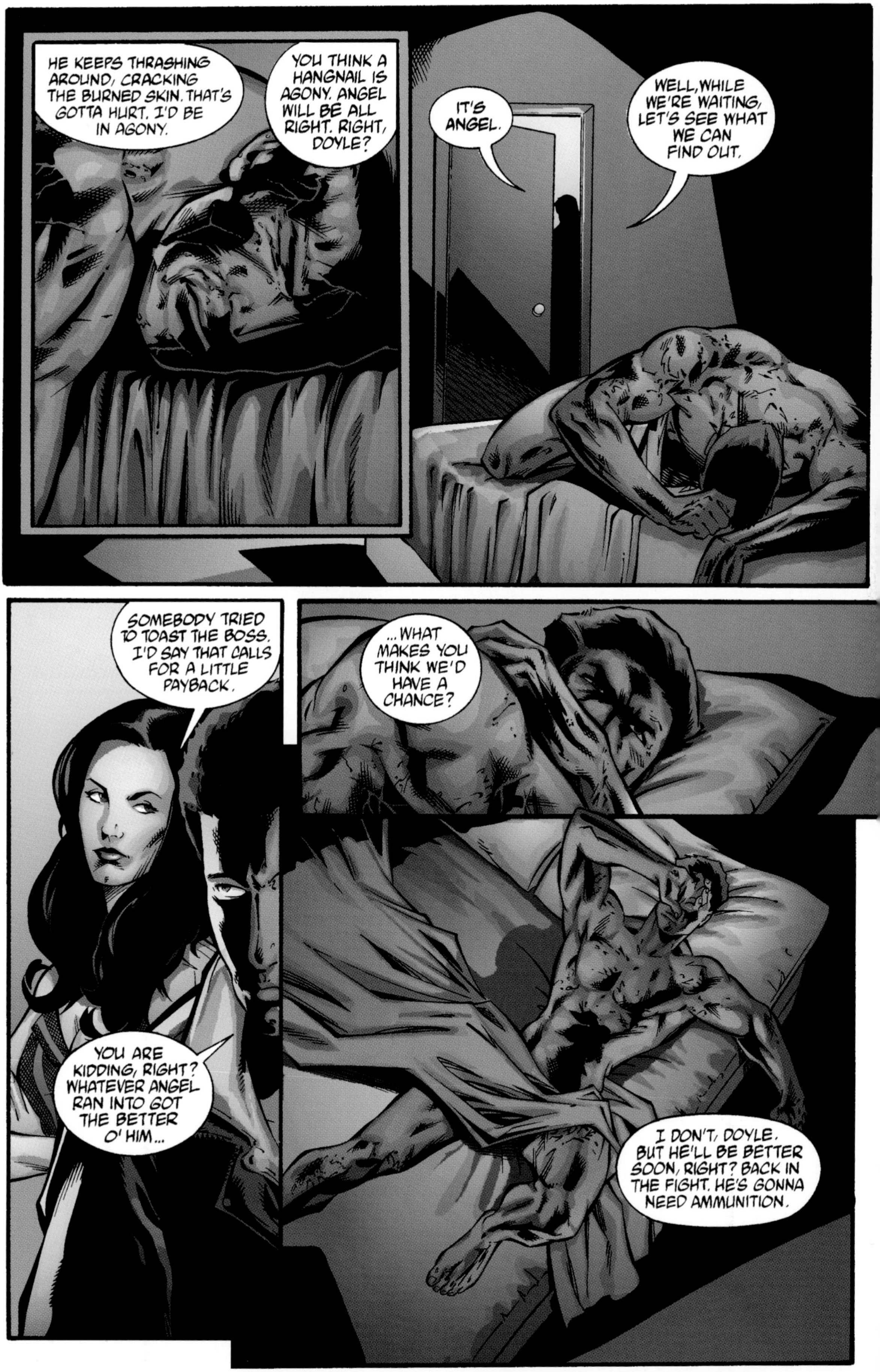
HE KEEPS THRASHING AROUND, CRACKING THE BURNED SKIN. THAT'S GOTTA HURT. I'D BE IN AGONY.
YOU THINK A HANGNAIL IS AGONY. ANGEL WILL BE ALL RIGHT. RIGHT, DOYLE?
IT'S ANGEL.
WELL, WHILE WE'RE WAITING, LET'S SEE WHAT WE CAN FIND OUT.
SOMEBODY TRIED TO TOAST THE BOSS. I'D SAY THAT CALLS FOR A LITTLE PAYBACK.
...WHAT MAKES YOU THINK WE'D HAVE A CHANCE?
YOU ARE KIDDING, RIGHT? WHATEVER ANGEL RAN INTO GOT THE BETTER O' HIM...
I DON'T, DOYLE. BUT HE'LL BE BETTER SOON, RIGHT? BACK IN THE FIGHT. HE'S GONNA NEED AMMUNITION.

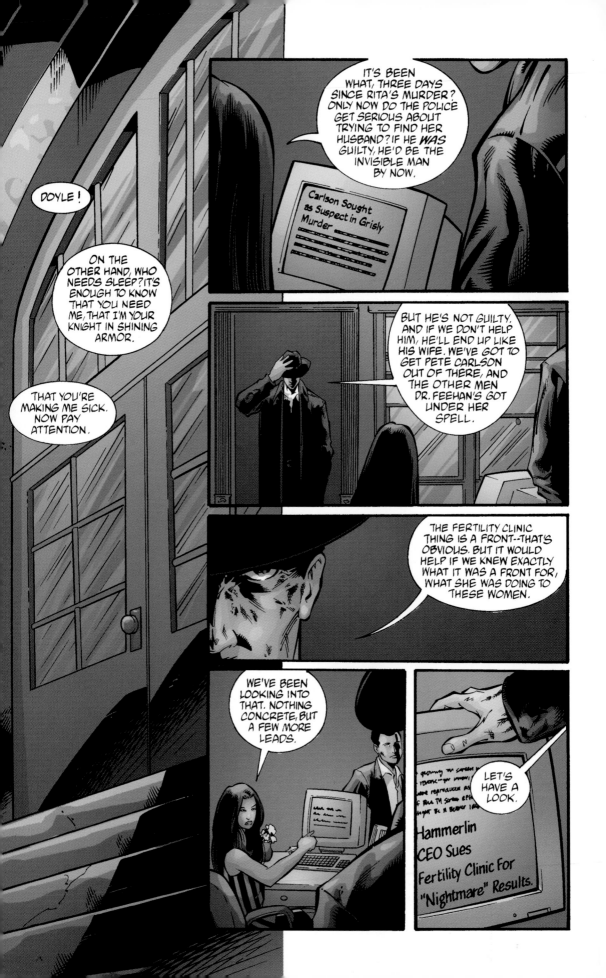

IT'S BEEN WHAT, THREE DAYS SINCE RITA'S MURDER? ONLY NOW DO THE POLICE GET SERIOUS ABOUT TRYING TO FIND HER HUSBAND? IF HE *WAS* GUILTY, HE'D BE THE INVISIBLE MAN BY NOW.

Carlson Sought as Suspect in Grisly Murder

DOYLE!

ON THE OTHER HAND, WHO NEEDS SLEEP? IT'S ENOUGH TO KNOW THAT YOU NEED ME, THAT I'M YOUR KNIGHT IN SHINING ARMOR.

BUT HE'S NOT GUILTY, AND IF WE DON'T HELP HIM, HE'LL END UP LIKE HIS WIFE. WE'VE GOT TO GET PETE CARLSON OUT OF THERE, AND THE OTHER MEN DR. FEEHAN'S GOT UNDER HER SPELL.

THAT YOU'RE MAKING ME SICK. NOW PAY ATTENTION.

THE FERTILITY CLINIC THING IS A FRONT--THAT'S OBVIOUS. BUT IT WOULD HELP IF WE KNEW EXACTLY WHAT IT WAS A FRONT FOR, WHAT SHE WAS DOING TO THESE WOMEN.

WE'VE BEEN LOOKING INTO THAT. NOTHING CONCRETE, BUT A FEW MORE LEADS.

LET'S HAVE A LOOK.

Hammerlin CEO Sues Fertility Clinic For "Nightmare" Results.

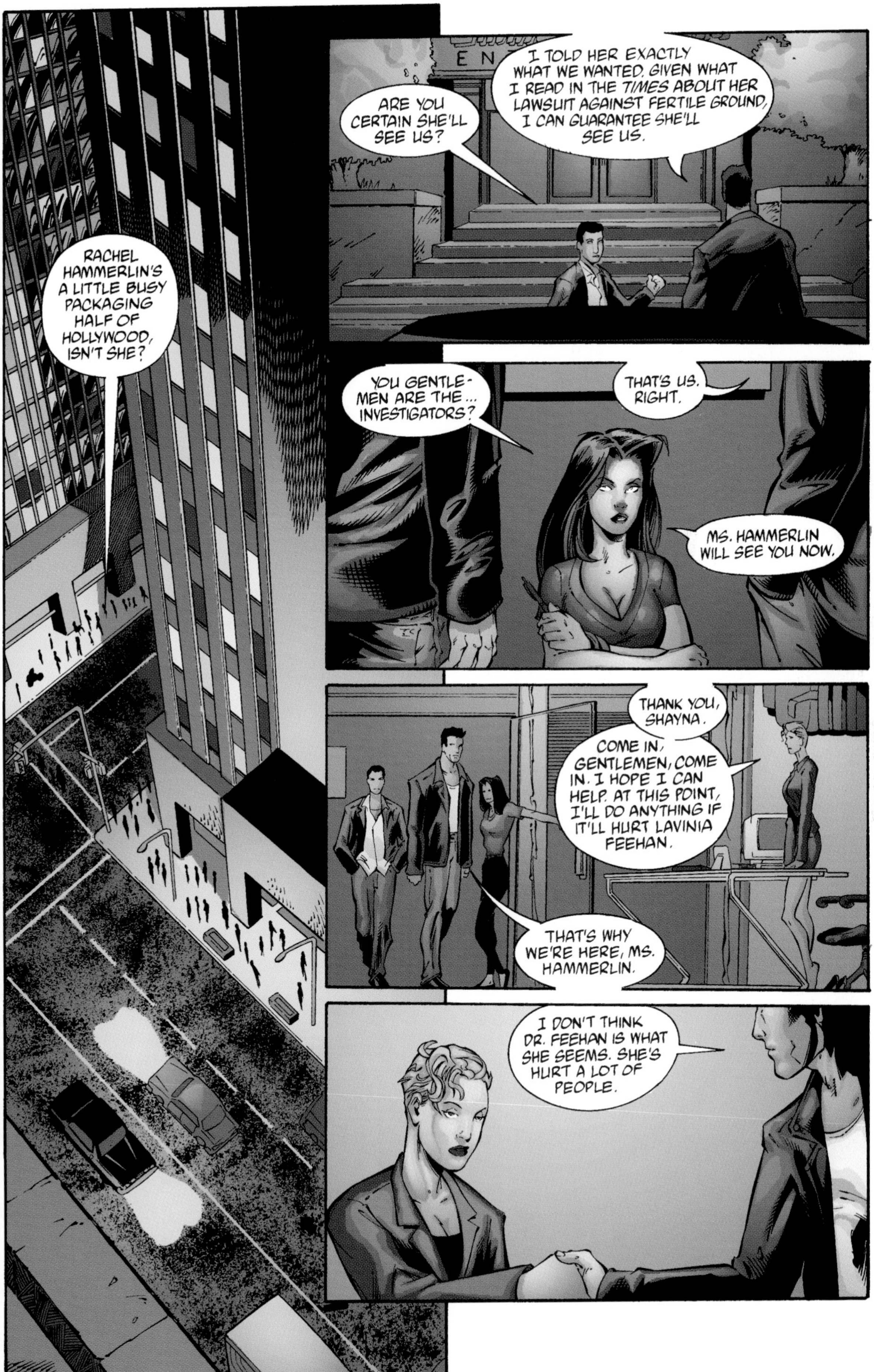
RACHEL HAMMERLIN'S A LITTLE BUSY PACKAGING HALF OF HOLLYWOOD, ISN'T SHE?
ARE YOU CERTAIN SHE'LL SEE US?
I TOLD HER EXACTLY WHAT WE WANTED. GIVEN WHAT I READ IN THE *TIMES* ABOUT HER LAWSUIT AGAINST FERTILE GROUND, I CAN GUARANTEE SHE'LL SEE US.
YOU GENTLEMEN ARE THE... INVESTIGATORS?
THAT'S US. RIGHT.
MS. HAMMERLIN WILL SEE YOU NOW.
THANK YOU, SHAYNA.
COME IN, GENTLEMEN, COME IN. I HOPE I CAN HELP. AT THIS POINT, I'LL DO ANYTHING IF IT'LL HURT LAVINIA FEEHAN.
THAT'S WHY WE'RE HERE, MS. HAMMERLIN.
I DON'T THINK DR. FEEHAN IS WHAT SHE SEEMS. SHE'S HURT A LOT OF PEOPLE.

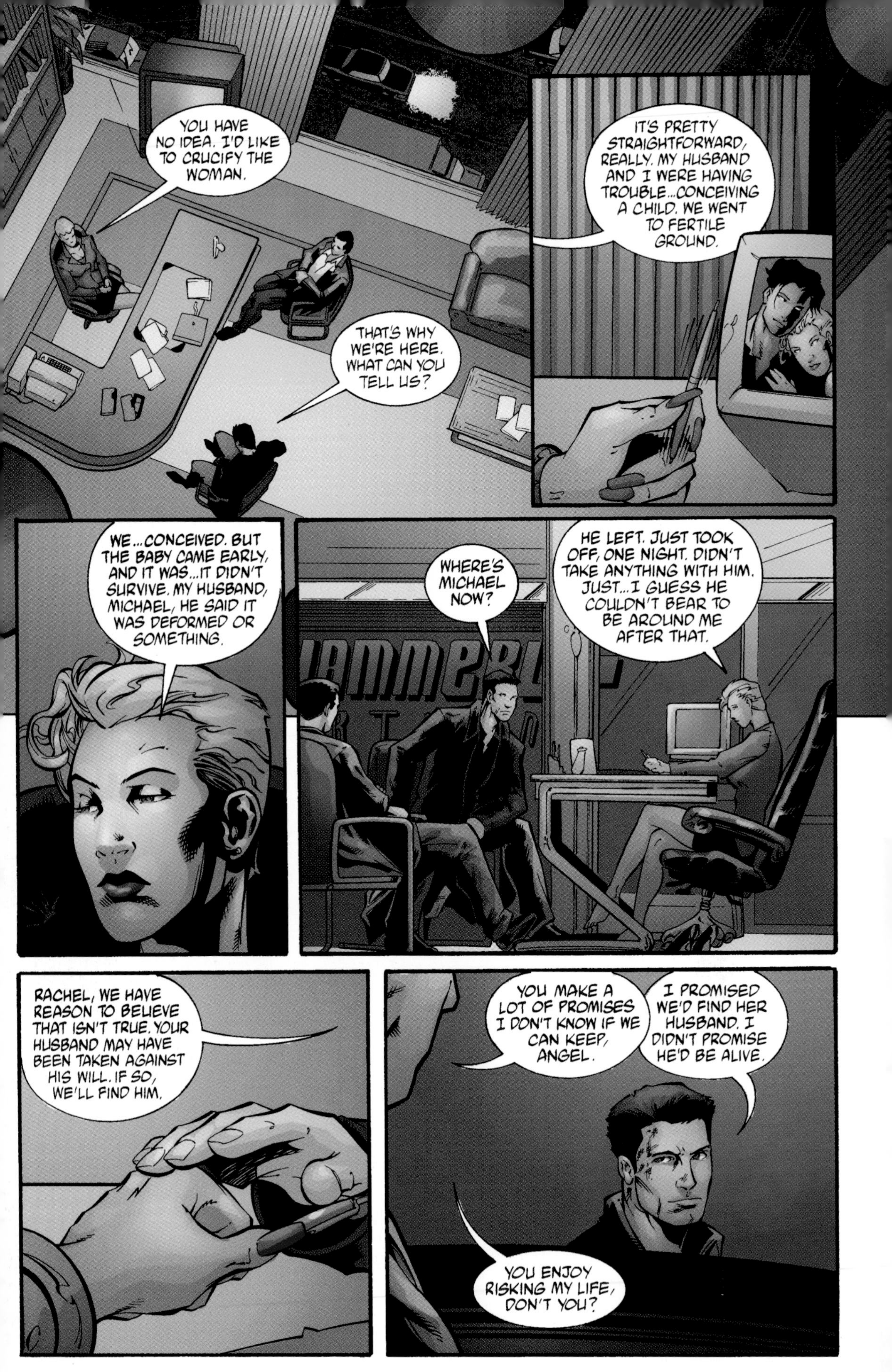
YOU HAVE NO IDEA. I'D LIKE TO CRUCIFY THE WOMAN.
THAT'S WHY WE'RE HERE. WHAT CAN YOU TELL US?
IT'S PRETTY STRAIGHTFORWARD, REALLY. MY HUSBAND AND I WERE HAVING TROUBLE...CONCEIVING A CHILD. WE WENT TO FERTILE GROUND.
WE...CONCEIVED. BUT THE BABY CAME EARLY, AND IT WAS...IT DIDN'T SURVIVE. MY HUSBAND, MICHAEL, HE SAID IT WAS DEFORMED OR SOMETHING.
WHERE'S MICHAEL NOW?
HE LEFT. JUST TOOK OFF, ONE NIGHT. DIDN'T TAKE ANYTHING WITH HIM. JUST...I GUESS HE COULDN'T BEAR TO BE AROUND ME AFTER THAT.
RACHEL, WE HAVE REASON TO BELIEVE THAT ISN'T TRUE. YOUR HUSBAND MAY HAVE BEEN TAKEN AGAINST HIS WILL. IF SO, WE'LL FIND HIM.
YOU MAKE A LOT OF PROMISES I DON'T KNOW IF WE CAN KEEP, ANGEL.
I PROMISED WE'D FIND HER HUSBAND. I DIDN'T PROMISE HE'D BE ALIVE.
YOU ENJOY RISKING MY LIFE, DON'T YOU?

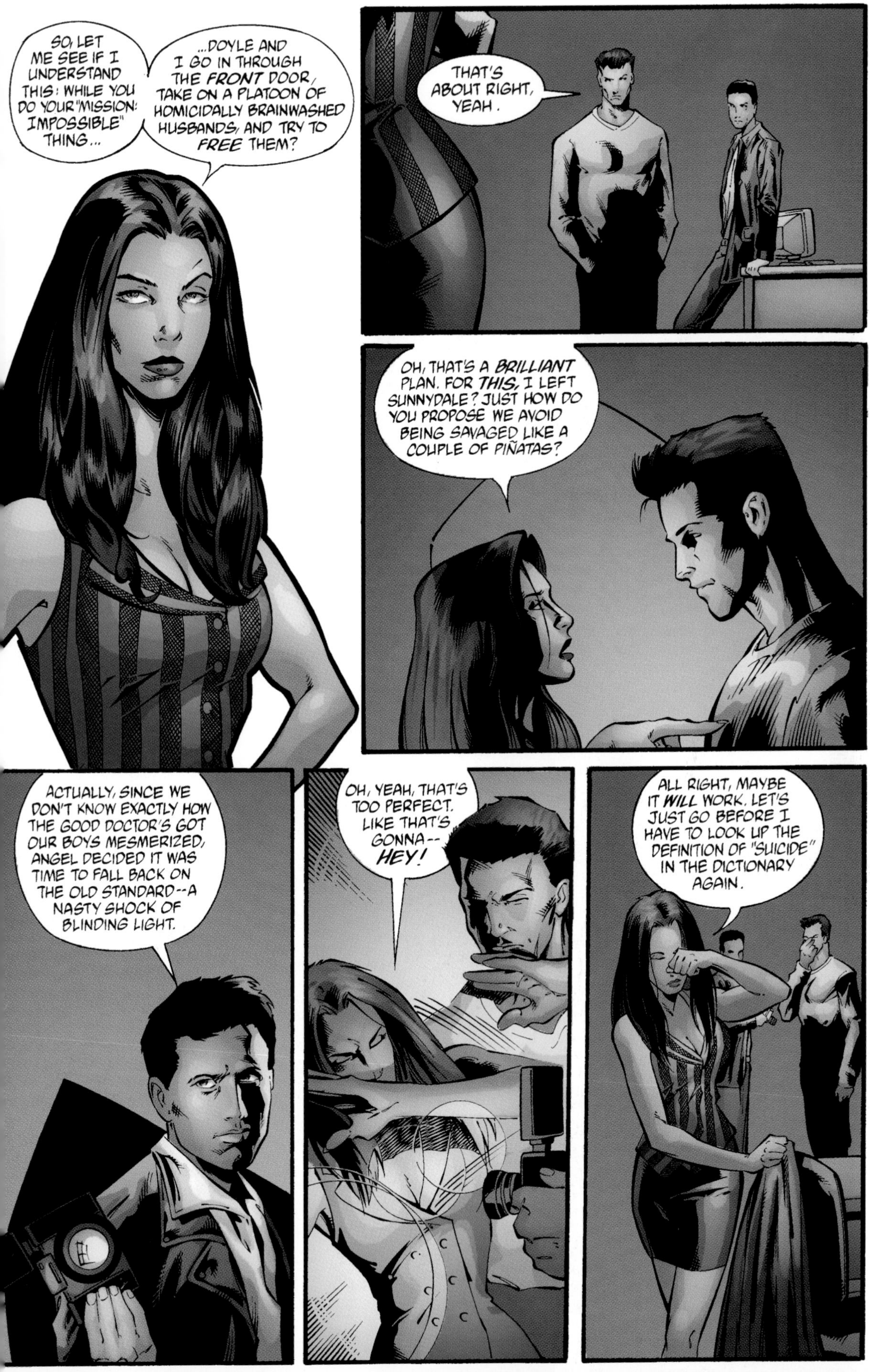
SO, LET ME SEE IF I UNDERSTAND THIS: WHILE YOU DO YOUR "MISSION: IMPOSSIBLE" THING...
...DOYLE AND I GO IN THROUGH THE *FRONT* DOOR, TAKE ON A PLATOON OF HOMICIDALLY BRAINWASHED HUSBANDS, AND TRY TO *FREE* THEM?
THAT'S ABOUT RIGHT, YEAH.
OH, THAT'S A *BRILLIANT* PLAN. FOR *THIS,* I LEFT SUNNYDALE? JUST HOW DO YOU PROPOSE WE AVOID BEING SAVAGED LIKE A COUPLE OF PIÑATAS?
ACTUALLY, SINCE WE DON'T KNOW EXACTLY HOW THE GOOD DOCTOR'S GOT OUR BOYS MESMERIZED, ANGEL DECIDED IT WAS TIME TO FALL BACK ON THE OLD STANDARD--A NASTY SHOCK OF BLINDING LIGHT.
OH, YEAH, THAT'S TOO PERFECT. LIKE THAT'S GONNA-- *HEY!*
ALL RIGHT, MAYBE IT *WILL* WORK. LET'S JUST GO BEFORE I HAVE TO LOOK UP THE DEFINITION OF "SUICIDE" IN THE DICTIONARY AGAIN.

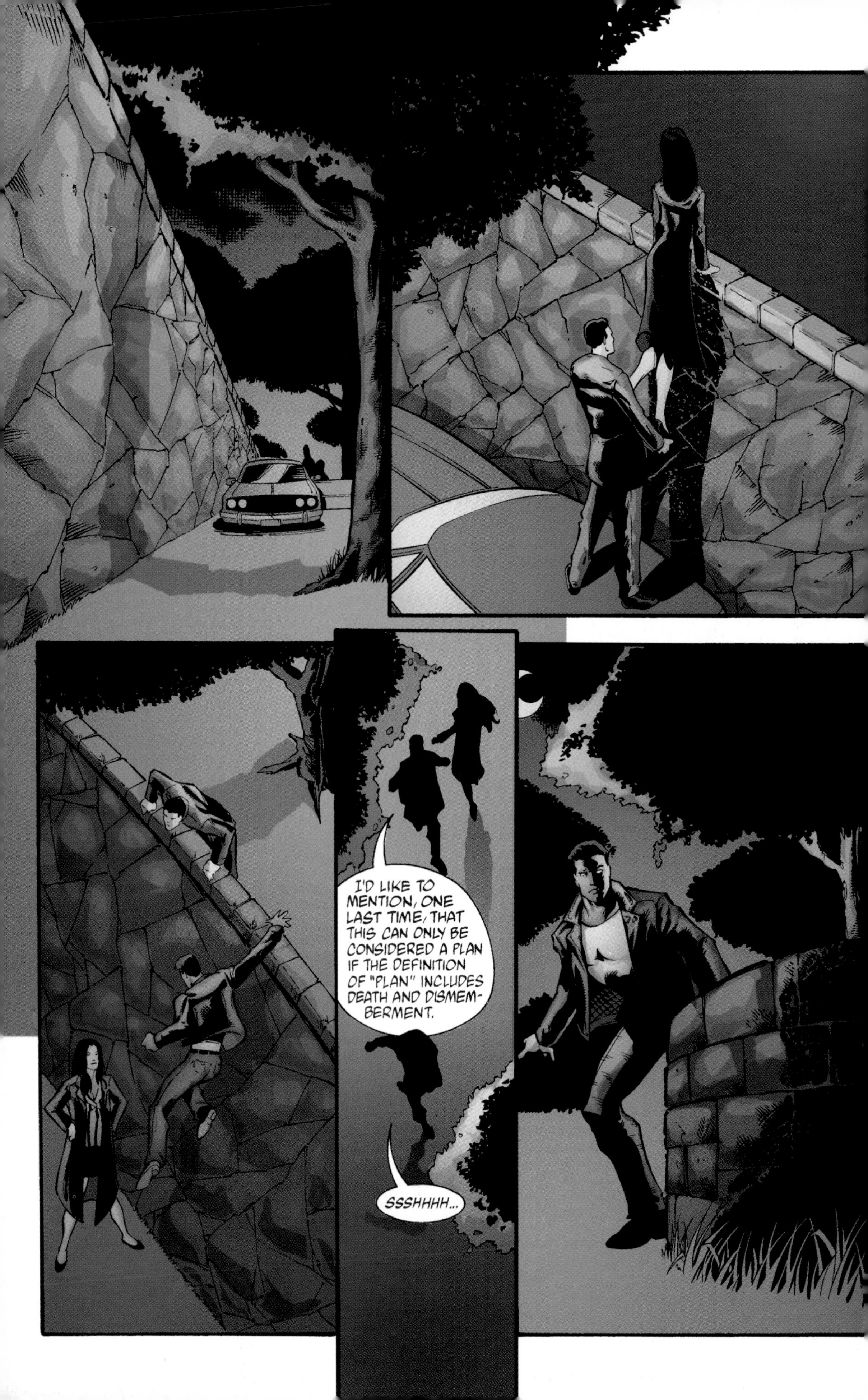
I'D LIKE TO MENTION, ONE LAST TIME, THAT THIS CAN ONLY BE CONSIDERED A PLAN IF THE DEFINITION OF "PLAN" INCLUDES DEATH AND DISMEMBERMENT.
SSSHHHH...

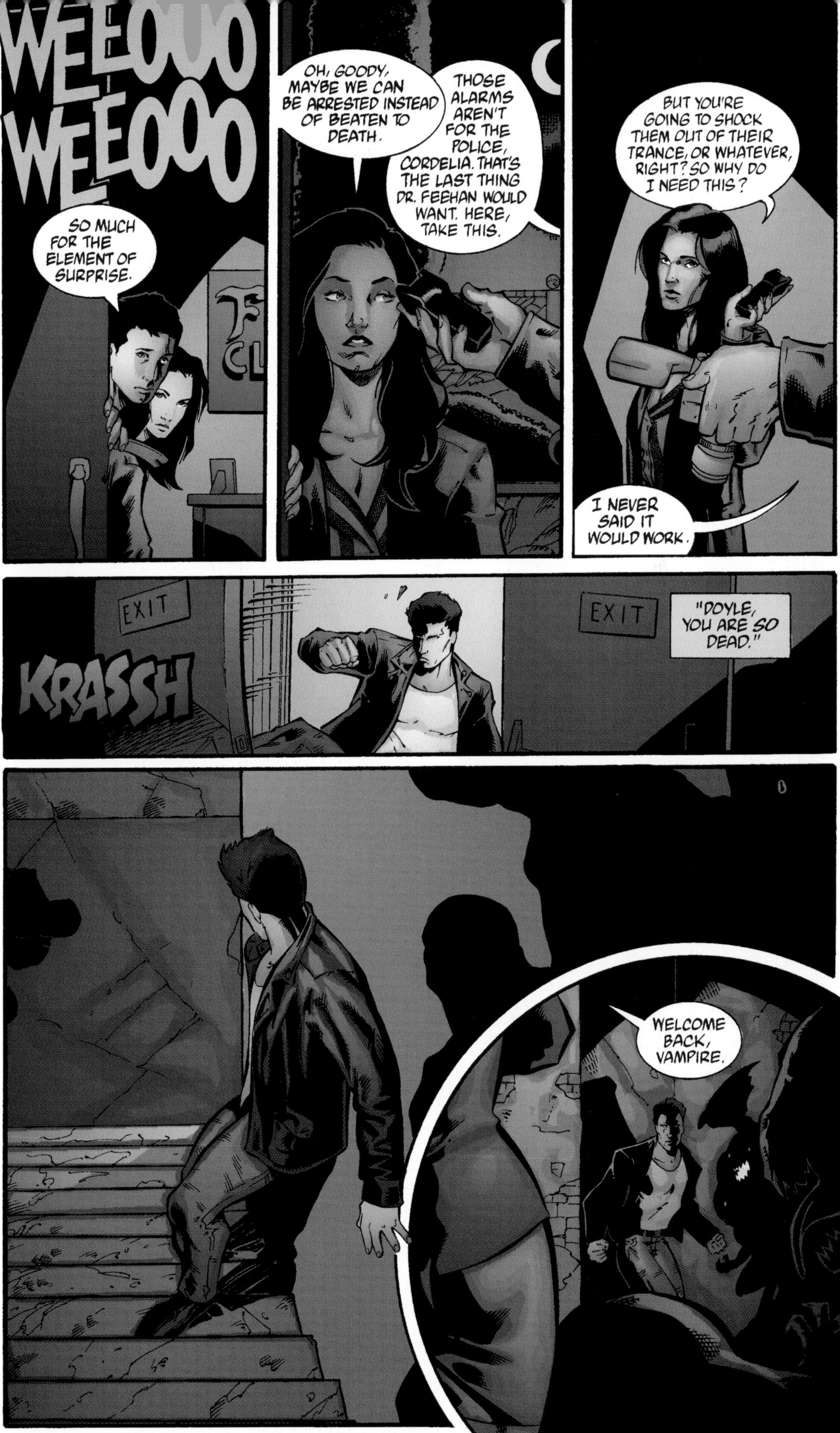
WEEOOO WEEOOO
SO MUCH FOR THE ELEMENT OF SURPRISE.
OH, GOODY, MAYBE WE CAN BE ARRESTED INSTEAD OF BEATEN TO DEATH.
THOSE ALARMS AREN'T FOR THE POLICE, CORDELIA. THAT'S THE LAST THING DR. FEEHAN WOULD WANT. HERE, TAKE THIS.
BUT YOU'RE GOING TO SHOCK THEM OUT OF THEIR TRANCE, OR WHATEVER, RIGHT? SO WHY DO I NEED THIS?
I NEVER SAID IT WOULD WORK.
EXIT
KRASSH
EXIT
"DOYLE, YOU ARE SO DEAD."
WELCOME BACK, VAMPIRE.

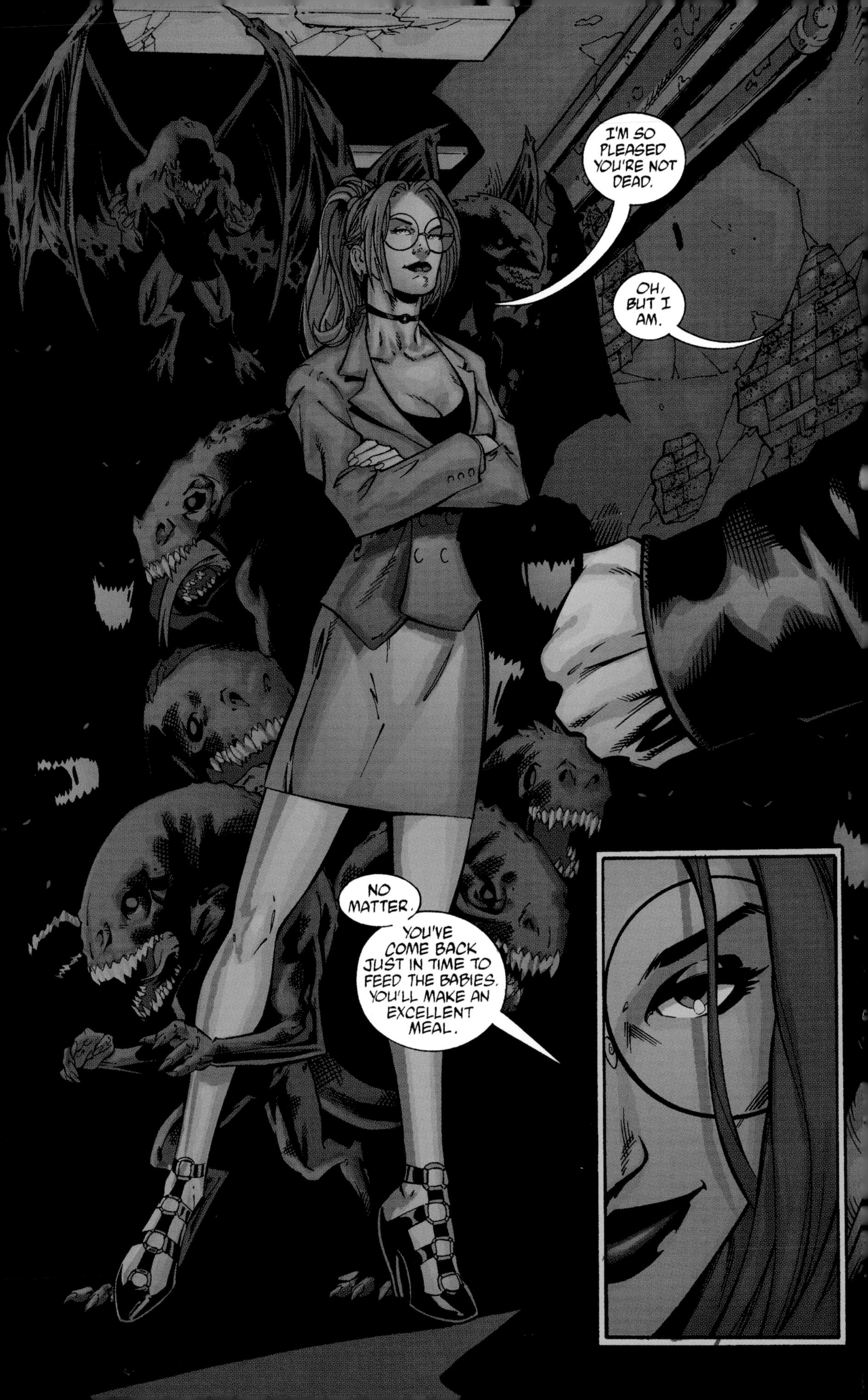
I'M SO PLEASED YOU'RE NOT DEAD.
OH, BUT I AM.
NO MATTER.
YOU'VE COME BACK JUST IN TIME TO FEED THE BABIES. YOU'LL MAKE AN EXCELLENT MEAL.

Cover by JEFF MATSUDA and JON SIBAL
Colors by GUY MAJOR

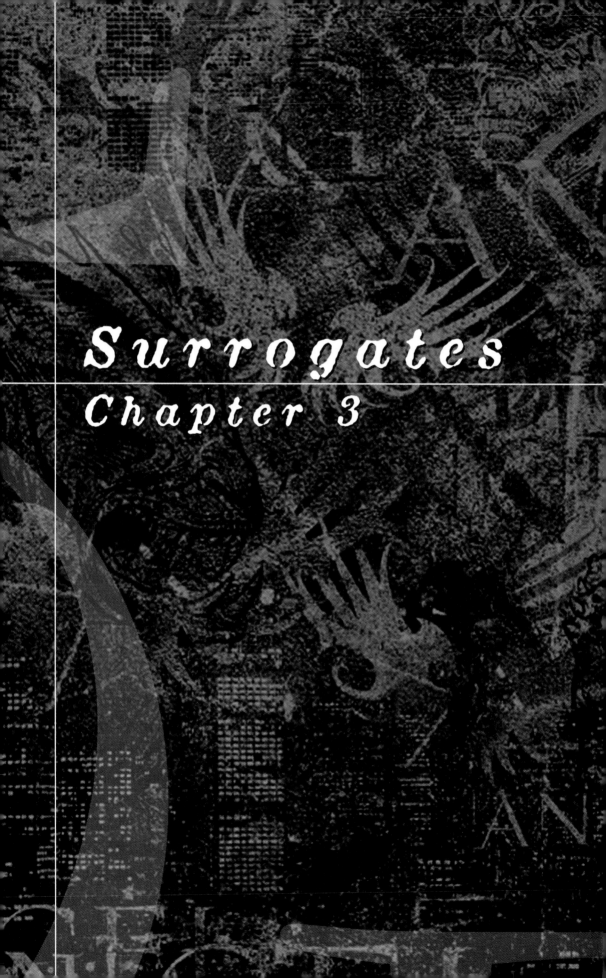

Surrogates
Chapter 3

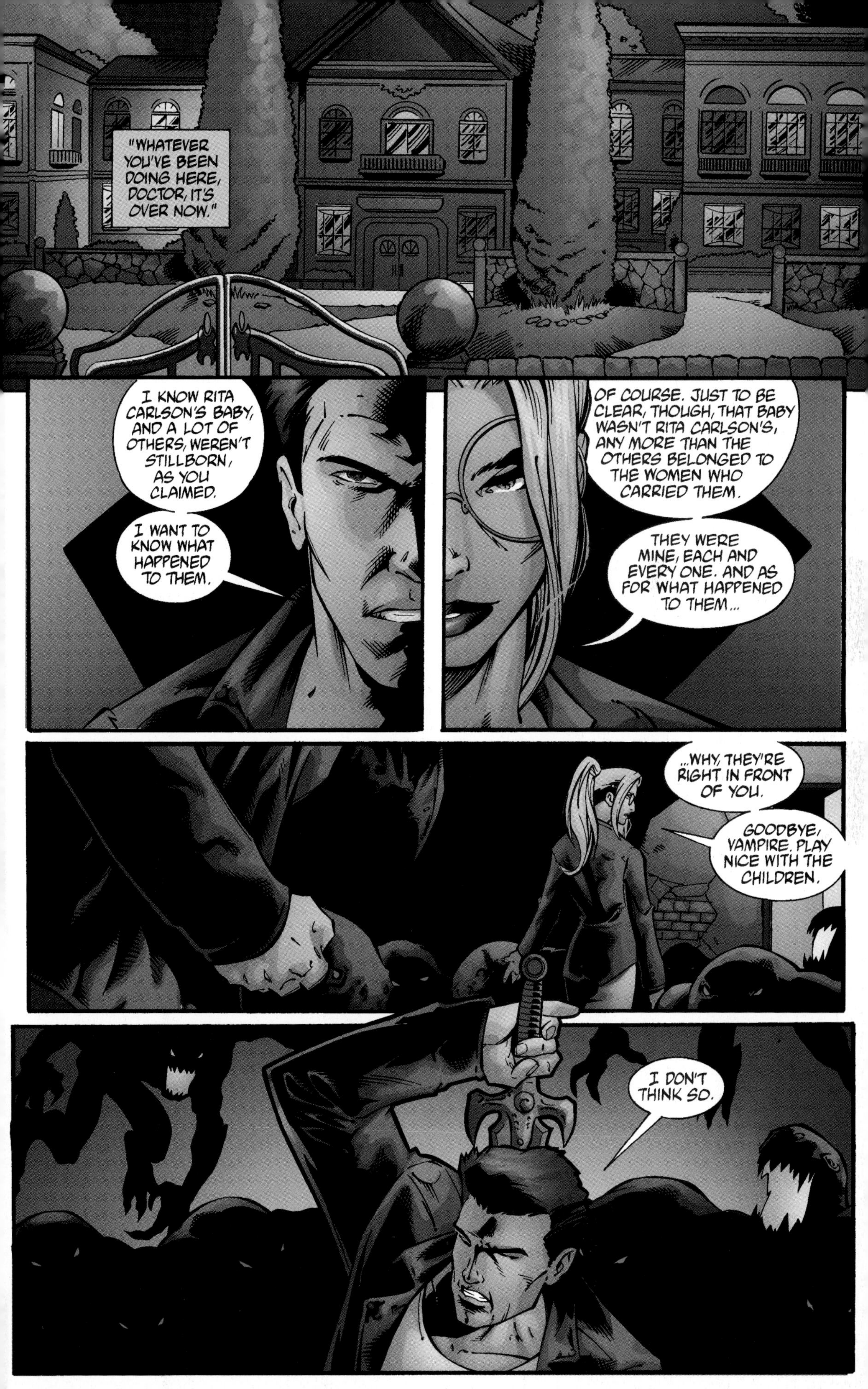
"WHATEVER YOU'VE BEEN DOING HERE, DOCTOR, IT'S OVER NOW."
I KNOW RITA CARLSON'S BABY, AND A LOT OF OTHERS, WEREN'T STILLBORN, AS YOU CLAIMED.
I WANT TO KNOW WHAT HAPPENED TO THEM.
OF COURSE. JUST TO BE CLEAR, THOUGH, THAT BABY WASN'T RITA CARLSON'S, ANY MORE THAN THE OTHERS BELONGED TO THE WOMEN WHO CARRIED THEM.
THEY WERE MINE, EACH AND EVERY ONE. AND AS FOR WHAT HAPPENED TO THEM...
...WHY, THEY'RE RIGHT IN FRONT OF YOU.
GOODBYE, VAMPIRE. PLAY NICE WITH THE CHILDREN.
I DON'T THINK SO.

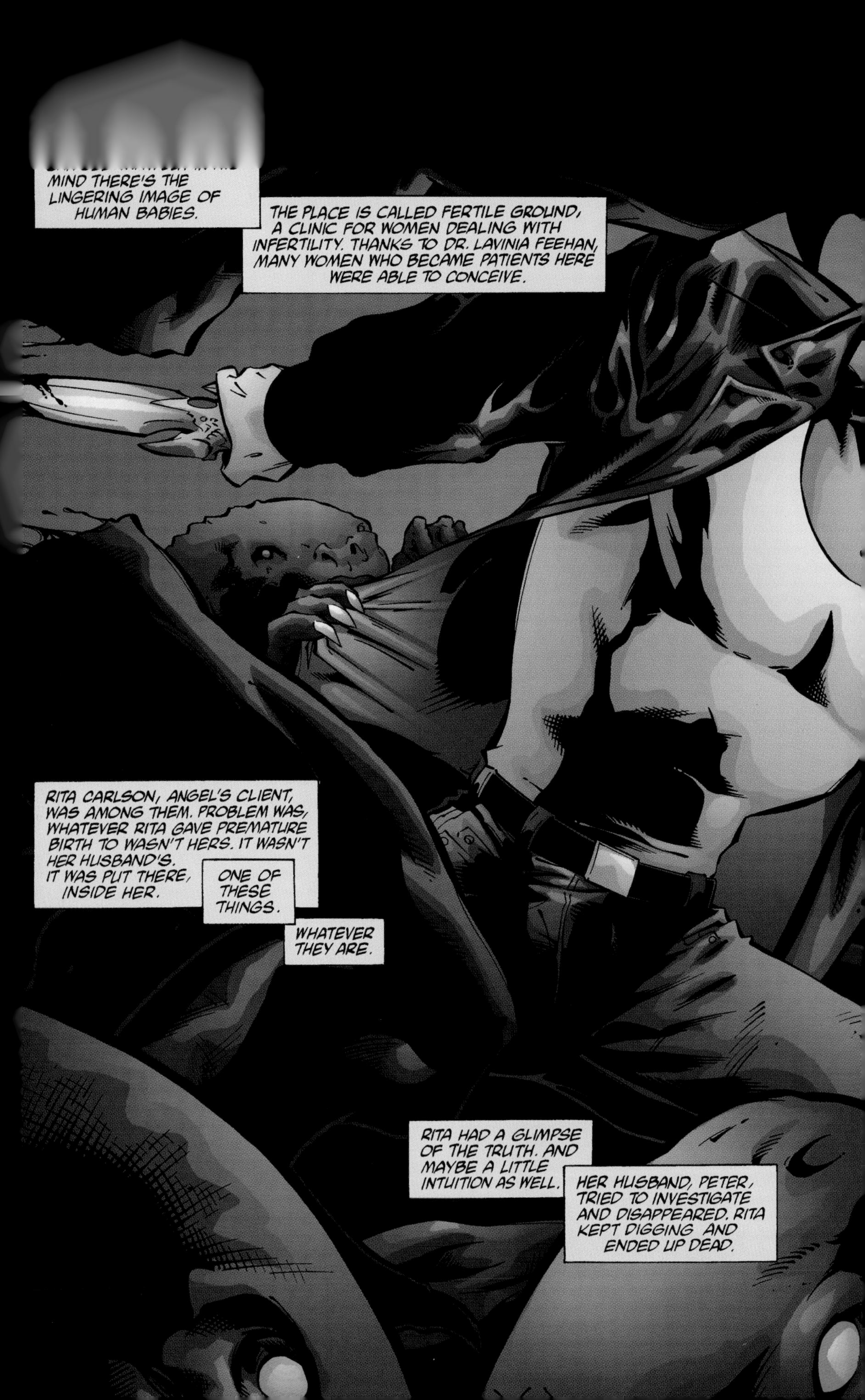
MIND THERE'S THE LINGERING IMAGE OF HUMAN BABIES.
THE PLACE IS CALLED FERTILE GROUND, A CLINIC FOR WOMEN DEALING WITH INFERTILITY. THANKS TO DR. LAVINIA FEEHAN, MANY WOMEN WHO BECAME PATIENTS HERE WERE ABLE TO CONCEIVE.
RITA CARLSON, ANGEL'S CLIENT, WAS AMONG THEM. PROBLEM WAS, WHATEVER RITA GAVE PREMATURE BIRTH TO WASN'T HERS. IT WASN'T HER HUSBAND'S. IT WAS PUT THERE, INSIDE HER.
ONE OF THESE THINGS.
WHATEVER THEY ARE.
RITA HAD A GLIMPSE OF THE TRUTH. AND MAYBE A LITTLE INTUITION AS WELL.
HER HUSBAND, PETER, TRIED TO INVESTIGATE AND DISAPPEARED. RITA KEPT DIGGING AND ENDED UP DEAD.

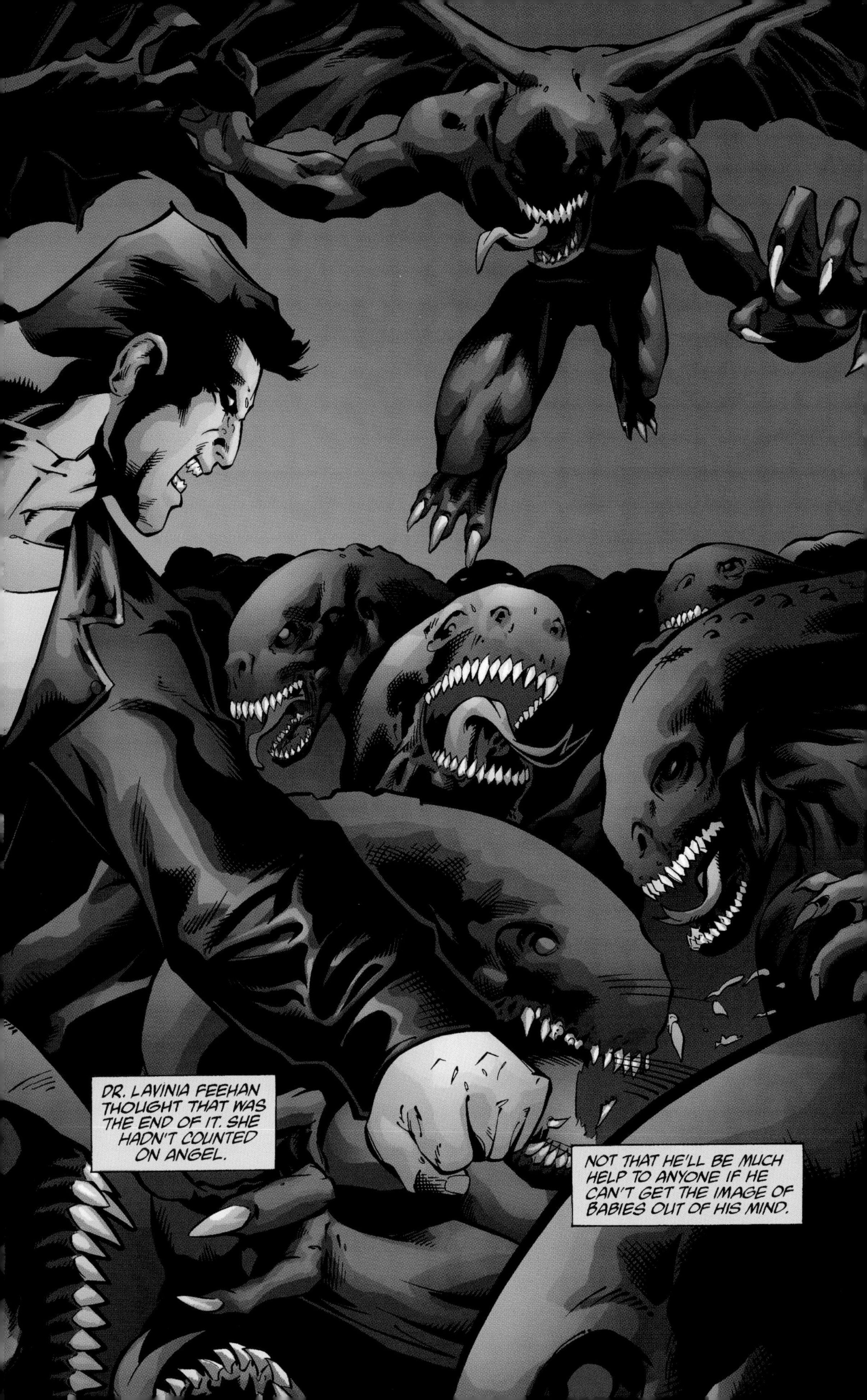
DR. LAVINIA FEEHAN THOUGHT THAT WAS THE END OF IT. SHE HADN'T COUNTED ON ANGEL.
NOT THAT HE'LL BE MUCH HELP TO ANYONE IF HE CAN'T GET THE IMAGE OF BABIES OUT OF HIS MIND.

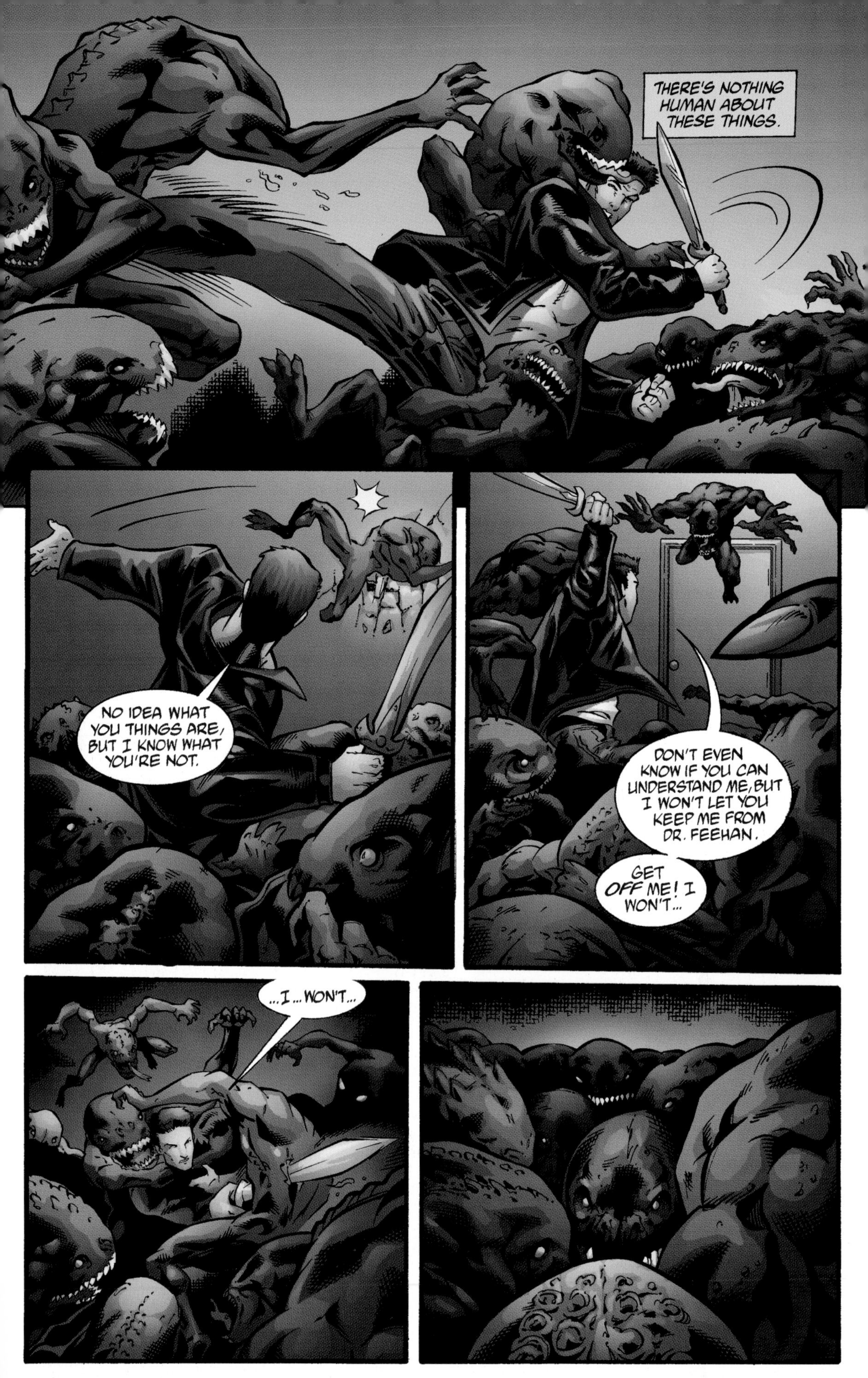
THERE'S NOTHING HUMAN ABOUT THESE THINGS.
NO IDEA WHAT YOU THINGS ARE, BUT I KNOW WHAT YOU'RE NOT.
DON'T EVEN KNOW IF YOU CAN UNDERSTAND ME, BUT I WON'T LET YOU KEEP ME FROM DR. FEEHAN.
GET OFF ME! I WON'T...
...I...WON'T...

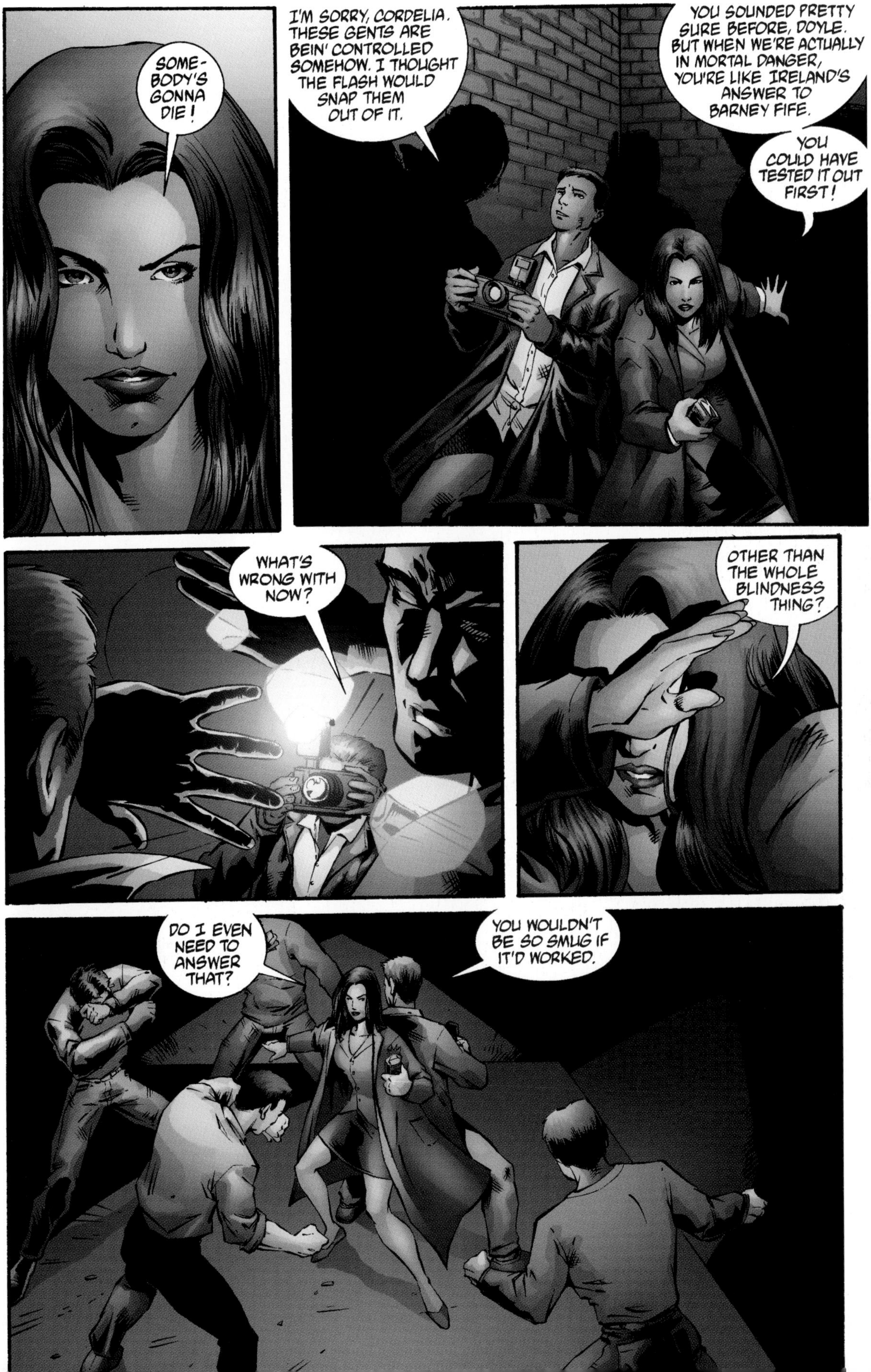
SOME-BODY'S GONNA DIE!
I'M SORRY, CORDELIA. THESE GENTS ARE BEIN' CONTROLLED SOMEHOW. I THOUGHT THE FLASH WOULD SNAP THEM OUT OF IT.
YOU SOUNDED PRETTY SURE BEFORE, DOYLE. BUT WHEN WE'RE ACTUALLY IN MORTAL DANGER, YOU'RE LIKE IRELAND'S ANSWER TO BARNEY FIFE.
YOU COULD HAVE TESTED IT OUT FIRST!
WHAT'S WRONG WITH NOW?
OTHER THAN THE WHOLE BLINDNESS THING?
DO I EVEN NEED TO ANSWER THAT?
YOU WOULDN'T BE SO SMUG IF IT'D WORKED.

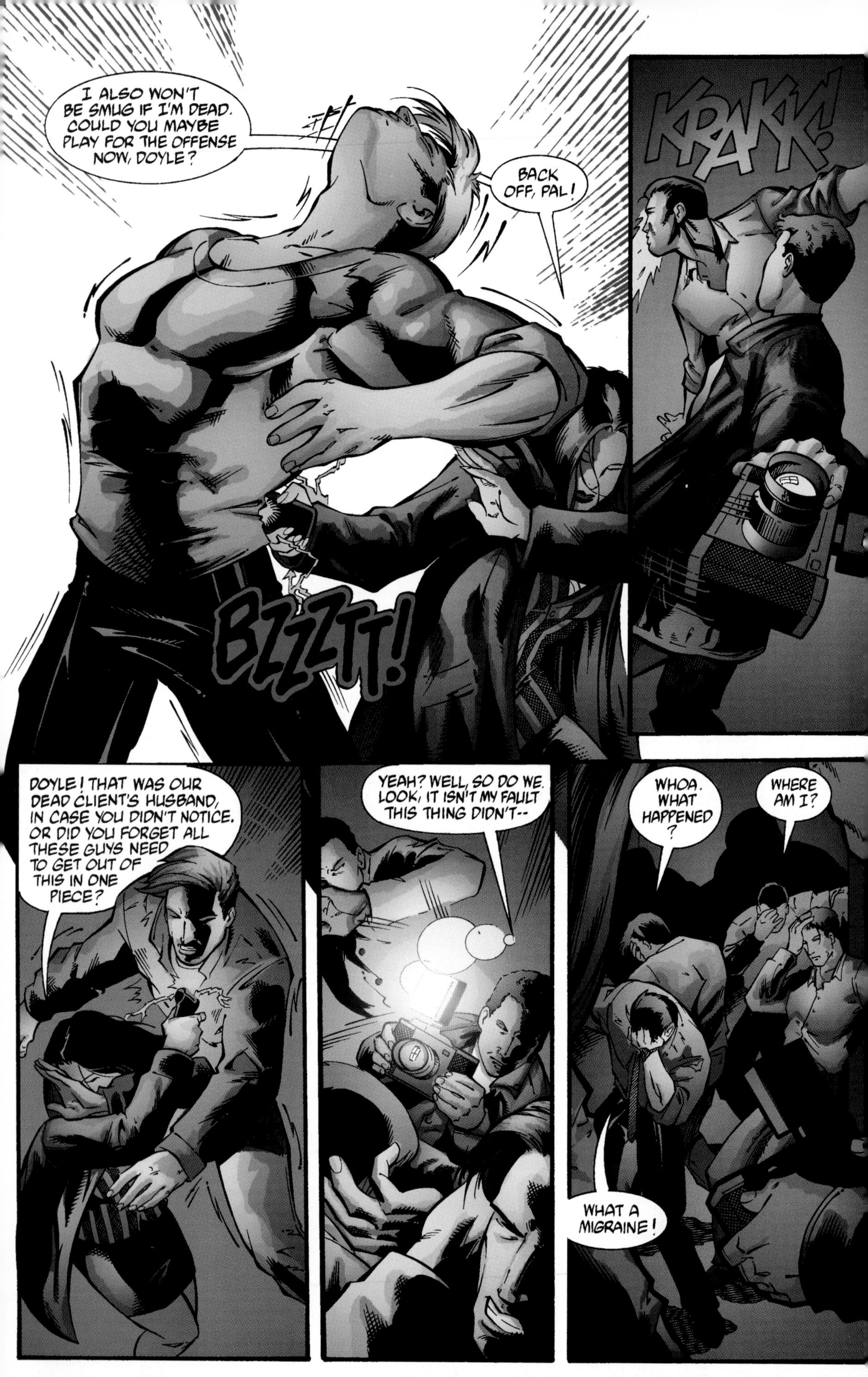
I ALSO WON'T BE SMUG IF I'M DEAD. COULD YOU MAYBE PLAY FOR THE OFFENSE NOW, DOYLE?
BACK OFF, PAL!
KRAKK!
BZZZTT!
DOYLE! THAT WAS OUR DEAD CLIENT'S HUSBAND, IN CASE YOU DIDN'T NOTICE. OR DID YOU FORGET ALL THESE GUYS NEED TO GET OUT OF THIS IN ONE PIECE?
YEAH? WELL, SO DO WE. LOOK, IT ISN'T MY FAULT THIS THING DIDN'T--
WHOA. WHAT HAPPENED?
WHERE AM I?
WHAT A MIGRAINE!

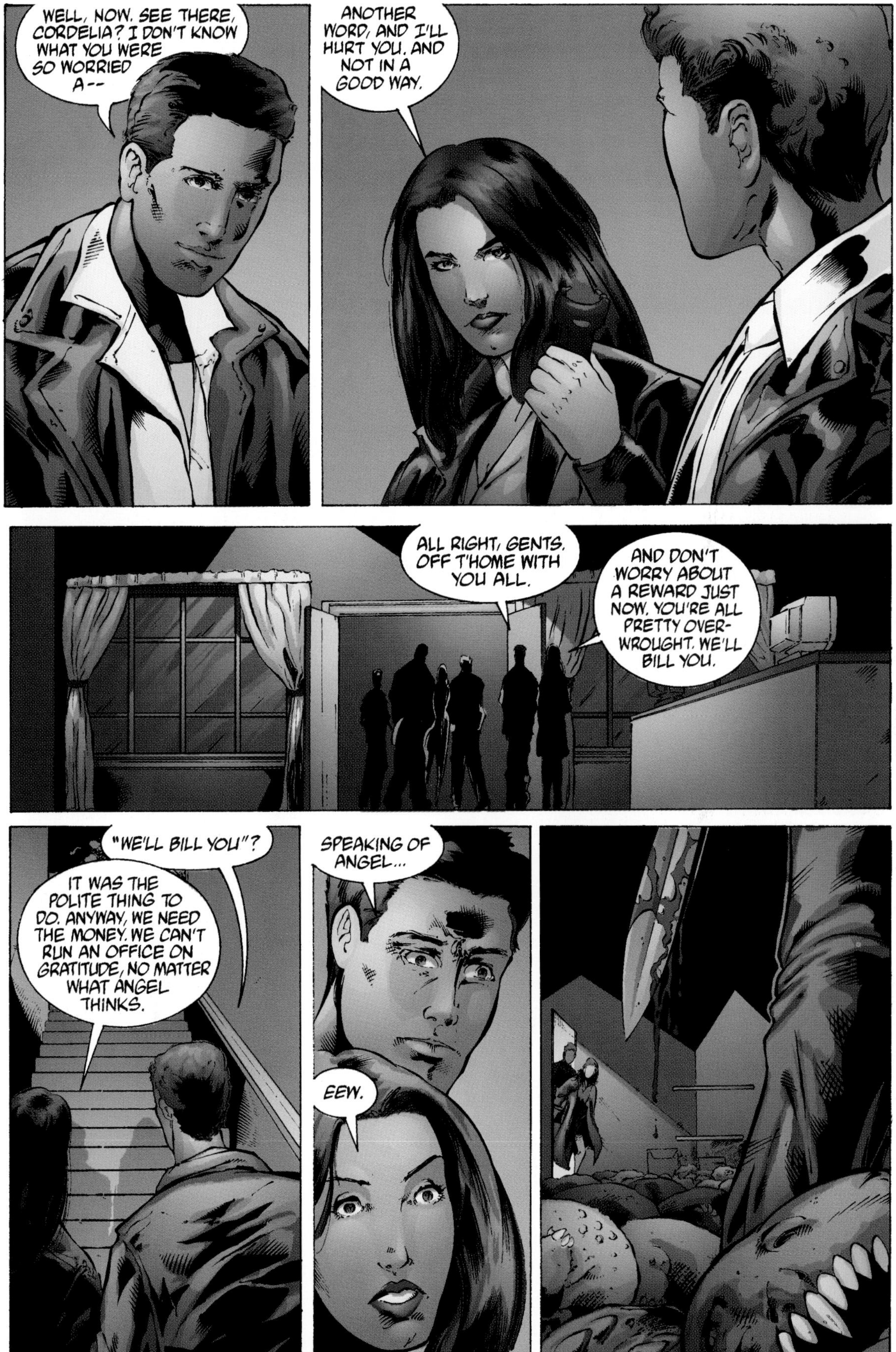
WELL, NOW. SEE THERE, CORDELIA? I DON'T KNOW WHAT YOU WERE SO WORRIED A--
ANOTHER WORD, AND I'LL HURT YOU. AND NOT IN A GOOD WAY.
ALL RIGHT, GENTS. OFF T'HOME WITH YOU ALL.
AND DON'T WORRY ABOUT A REWARD JUST NOW. YOU'RE ALL PRETTY OVER-WROUGHT. WE'LL BILL YOU.
"WE'LL BILL YOU"?
IT WAS THE POLITE THING TO DO. ANYWAY, WE NEED THE MONEY. WE CAN'T RUN AN OFFICE ON GRATITUDE, NO MATTER WHAT ANGEL THINKS.
SPEAKING OF ANGEL...
EEW.

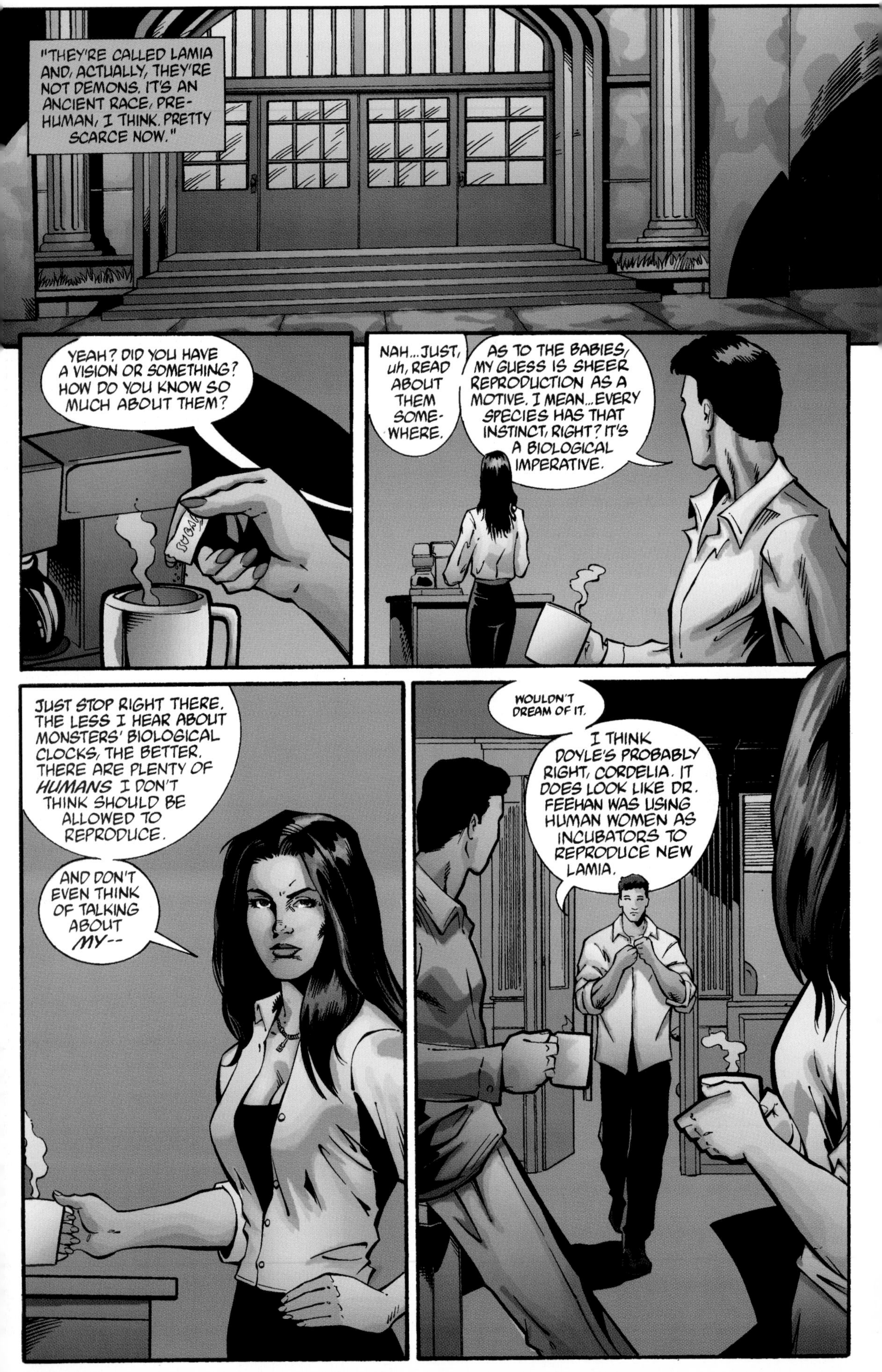
"THEY'RE CALLED LAMIA AND, ACTUALLY, THEY'RE NOT DEMONS. IT'S AN ANCIENT RACE, PRE-HUMAN, I THINK. PRETTY SCARCE NOW."
YEAH? DID YOU HAVE A VISION OR SOMETHING? HOW DO YOU KNOW SO MUCH ABOUT THEM?
NAH... JUST, uh, READ ABOUT THEM SOMEWHERE.
AS TO THE BABIES, MY GUESS IS SHEER REPRODUCTION AS A MOTIVE. I MEAN... EVERY SPECIES HAS THAT INSTINCT, RIGHT? IT'S A BIOLOGICAL IMPERATIVE.
JUST STOP RIGHT THERE. THE LESS I HEAR ABOUT MONSTERS' BIOLOGICAL CLOCKS, THE BETTER. THERE ARE PLENTY OF HUMANS I DON'T THINK SHOULD BE ALLOWED TO REPRODUCE.
AND DON'T EVEN THINK OF TALKING ABOUT MY--
WOULDN'T DREAM OF IT.
I THINK DOYLE'S PROBABLY RIGHT, CORDELIA. IT DOES LOOK LIKE DR. FEEHAN WAS USING HUMAN WOMEN AS INCUBATORS TO REPRODUCE NEW LAMIA.

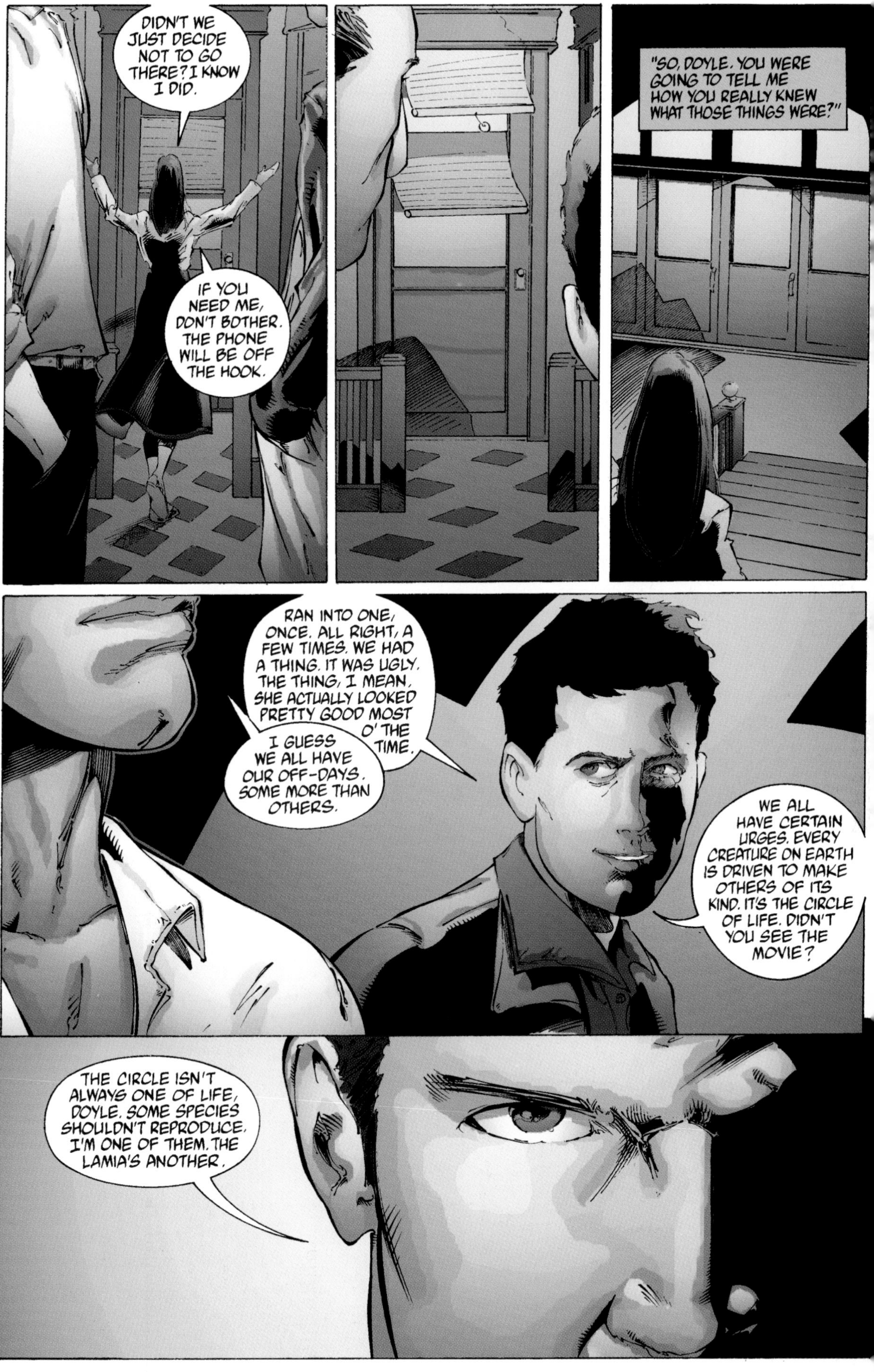
DIDN'T WE JUST DECIDE NOT TO GO THERE? I KNOW I DID.
IF YOU NEED ME, DON'T BOTHER. THE PHONE WILL BE OFF THE HOOK.
"SO, DOYLE. YOU WERE GOING TO TELL ME HOW YOU REALLY KNEW WHAT THOSE THINGS WERE?"
RAN INTO ONE, ONCE. ALL RIGHT, A FEW TIMES. WE HAD A THING. IT WAS UGLY. THE THING, I MEAN, SHE ACTUALLY LOOKED PRETTY GOOD MOST O' THE TIME.
I GUESS WE ALL HAVE OUR OFF-DAYS. SOME MORE THAN OTHERS.
WE ALL HAVE CERTAIN URGES. EVERY CREATURE ON EARTH IS DRIVEN TO MAKE OTHERS OF ITS KIND. IT'S THE CIRCLE OF LIFE. DIDN'T YOU SEE THE MOVIE?
THE CIRCLE ISN'T ALWAYS ONE OF LIFE, DOYLE. SOME SPECIES SHOULDN'T REPRODUCE. I'M ONE OF THEM. THE LAMIA'S ANOTHER.

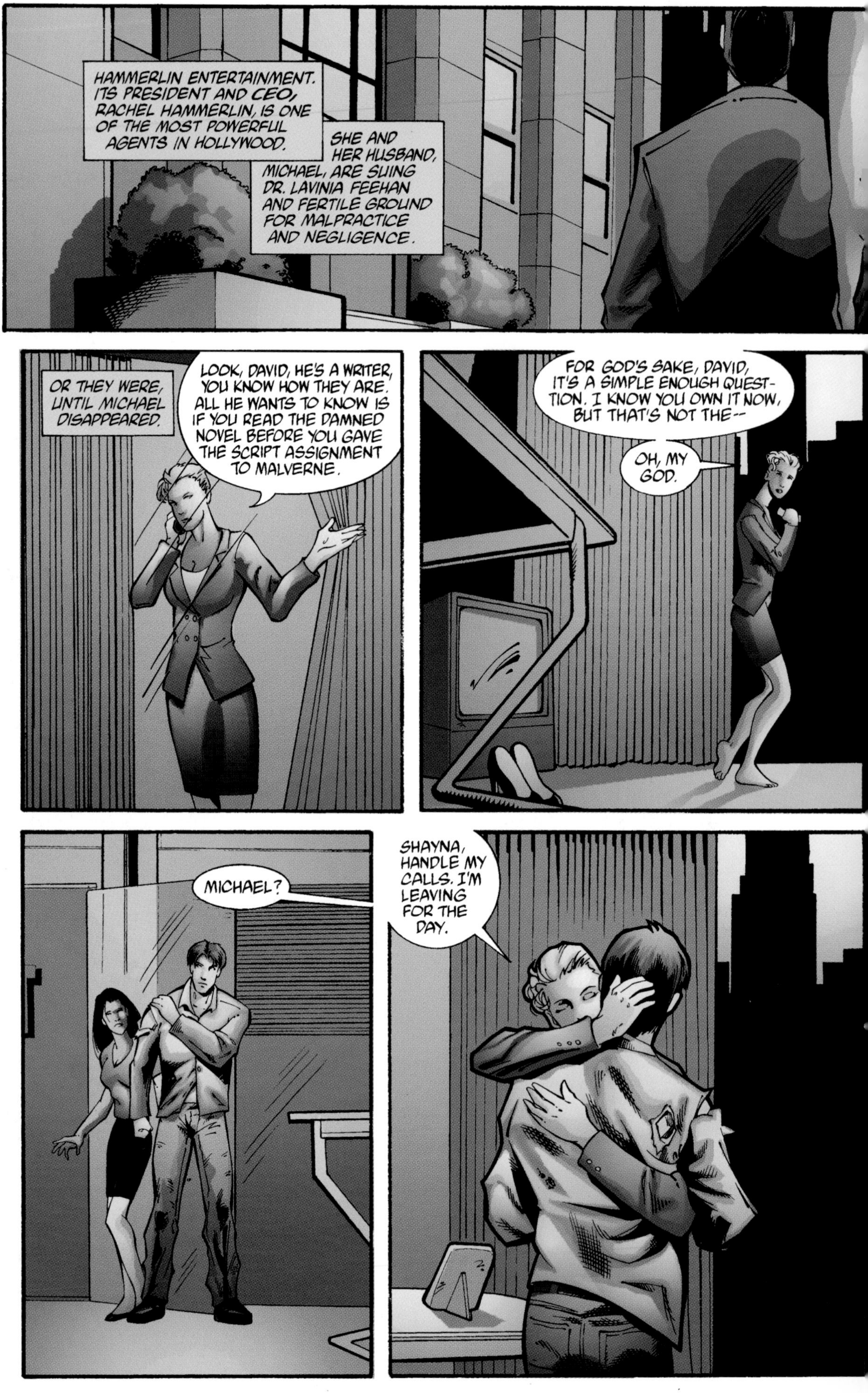
HAMMERLIN ENTERTAINMENT. ITS PRESIDENT AND CEO, RACHEL HAMMERLIN, IS ONE OF THE MOST POWERFUL AGENTS IN HOLLYWOOD.
SHE AND HER HUSBAND, MICHAEL, ARE SUING DR. LAVINIA FEEHAN AND FERTILE GROUND FOR MALPRACTICE AND NEGLIGENCE.
OR THEY WERE, UNTIL MICHAEL DISAPPEARED.
LOOK, DAVID, HE'S A WRITER, YOU KNOW HOW THEY ARE. ALL HE WANTS TO KNOW IS IF YOU READ THE DAMNED NOVEL BEFORE YOU GAVE THE SCRIPT ASSIGNMENT TO MALVERNE.
FOR GOD'S SAKE, DAVID, IT'S A SIMPLE ENOUGH QUESTION. I KNOW YOU OWN IT NOW, BUT THAT'S NOT THE--
OH, MY GOD.
MICHAEL?
SHAYNA, HANDLE MY CALLS. I'M LEAVING FOR THE DAY.

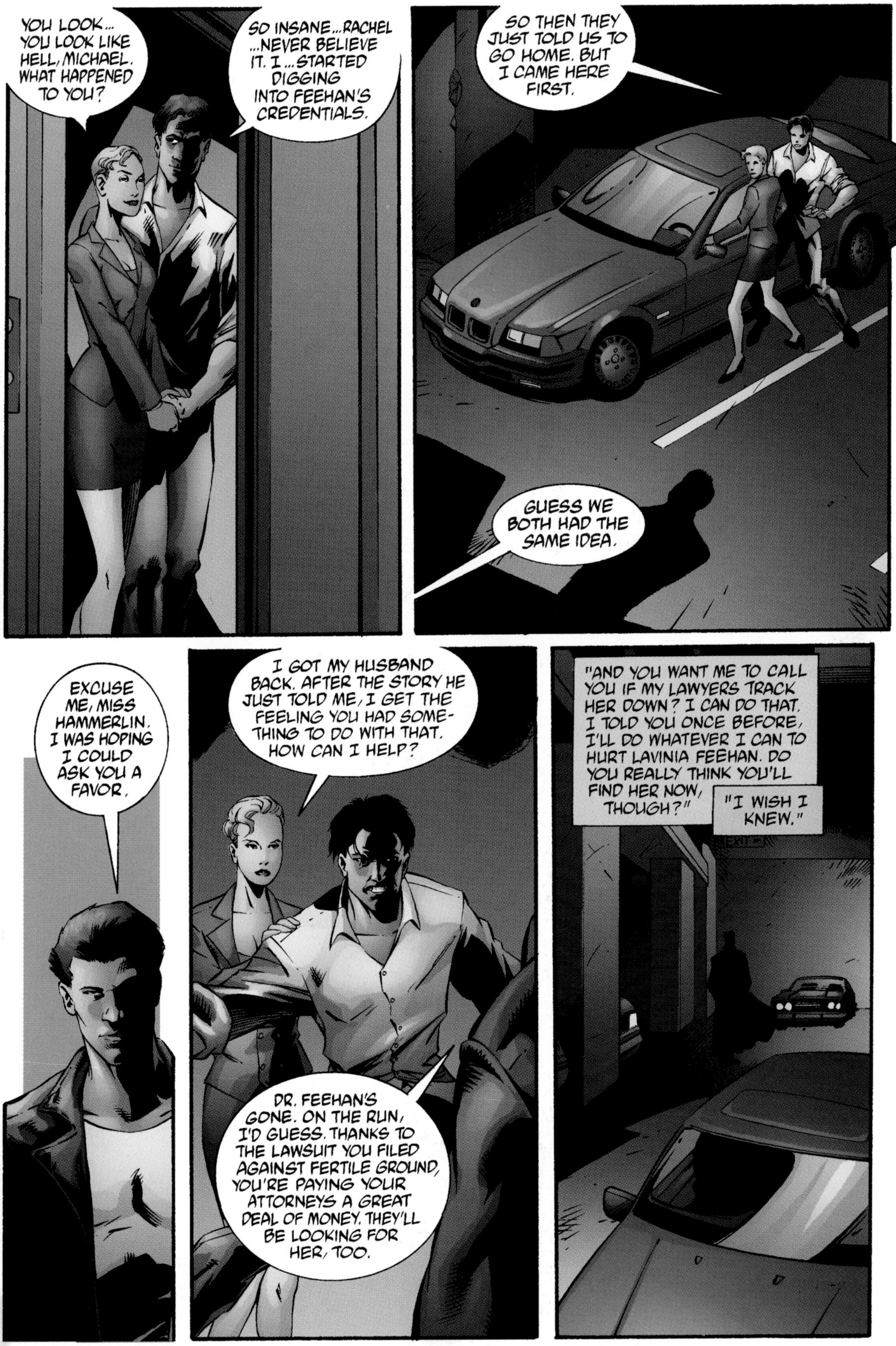
YOU LOOK... YOU LOOK LIKE HELL, MICHAEL. WHAT HAPPENED TO YOU?
SO INSANE...RACHEL ...NEVER BELIEVE IT. I ...STARTED DIGGING INTO FEEHAN'S CREDENTIALS.
SO THEN THEY JUST TOLD US TO GO HOME. BUT I CAME HERE FIRST.
GUESS WE BOTH HAD THE SAME IDEA.
EXCUSE ME, MISS HAMMERLIN. I WAS HOPING I COULD ASK YOU A FAVOR.
I GOT MY HUSBAND BACK. AFTER THE STORY HE JUST TOLD ME, I GET THE FEELING YOU HAD SOMETHING TO DO WITH THAT. HOW CAN I HELP?
DR. FEEHAN'S GONE. ON THE RUN, I'D GUESS. THANKS TO THE LAWSUIT YOU FILED AGAINST FERTILE GROUND, YOU'RE PAYING YOUR ATTORNEYS A GREAT DEAL OF MONEY. THEY'LL BE LOOKING FOR HER, TOO.
"AND YOU WANT ME TO CALL YOU IF MY LAWYERS TRACK HER DOWN? I CAN DO THAT. I TOLD YOU ONCE BEFORE, I'LL DO WHATEVER I CAN TO HURT LAVINIA FEEHAN. DO YOU REALLY THINK YOU'LL FIND HER NOW, THOUGH?"
"I WISH I KNEW."

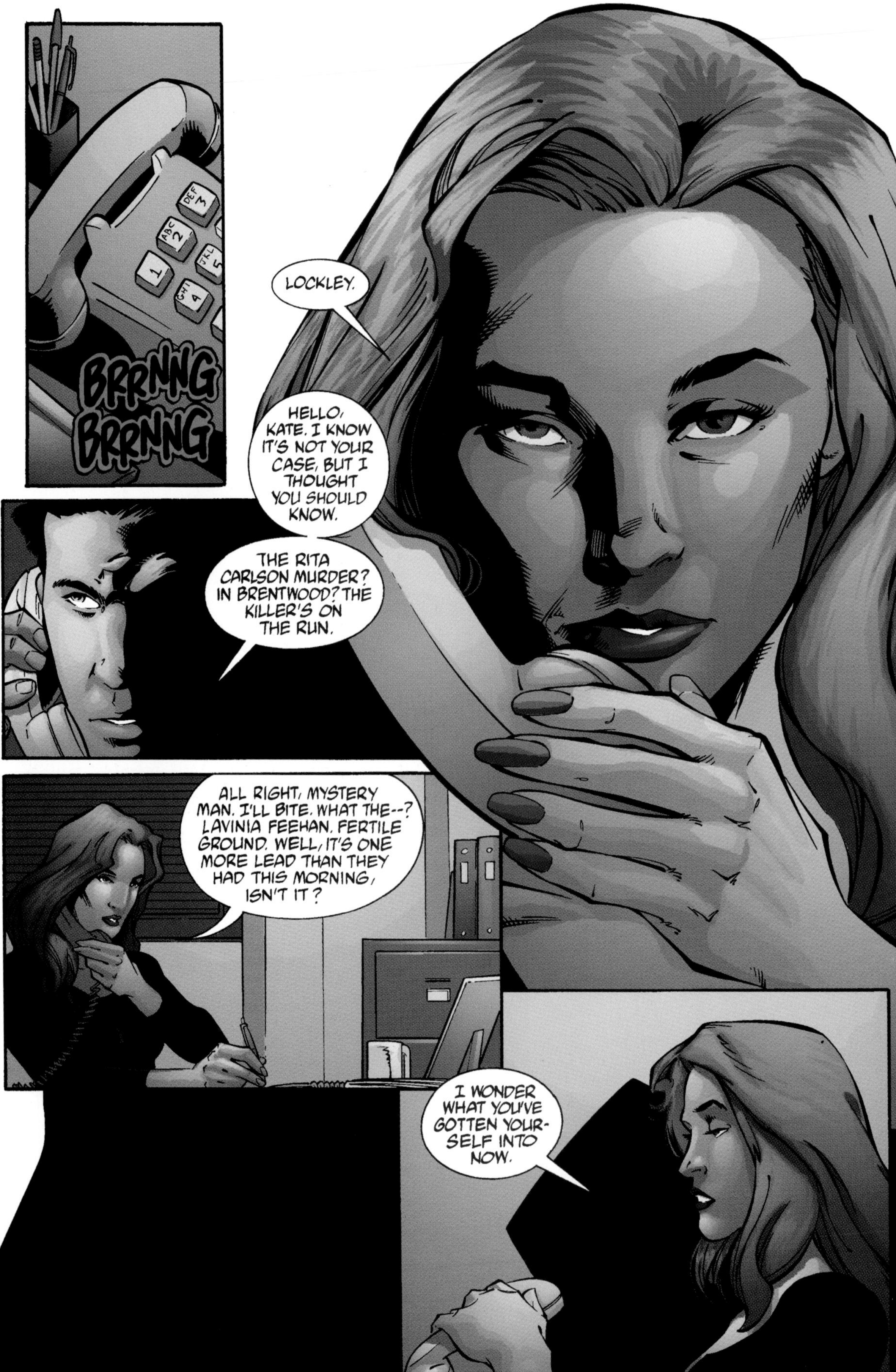
BRRNNG
BRRNNG
LOCKLEY.
HELLO, KATE. I KNOW IT'S NOT YOUR CASE, BUT I THOUGHT YOU SHOULD KNOW.
THE RITA CARLSON MURDER? IN BRENTWOOD? THE KILLER'S ON THE RUN.
ALL RIGHT, MYSTERY MAN. I'LL BITE. WHAT THE--? LAVINIA FEEHAN. FERTILE GROUND. WELL, IT'S ONE MORE LEAD THAN THEY HAD THIS MORNING, ISN'T IT?
I WONDER WHAT YOU'VE GOTTEN YOURSELF INTO NOW.

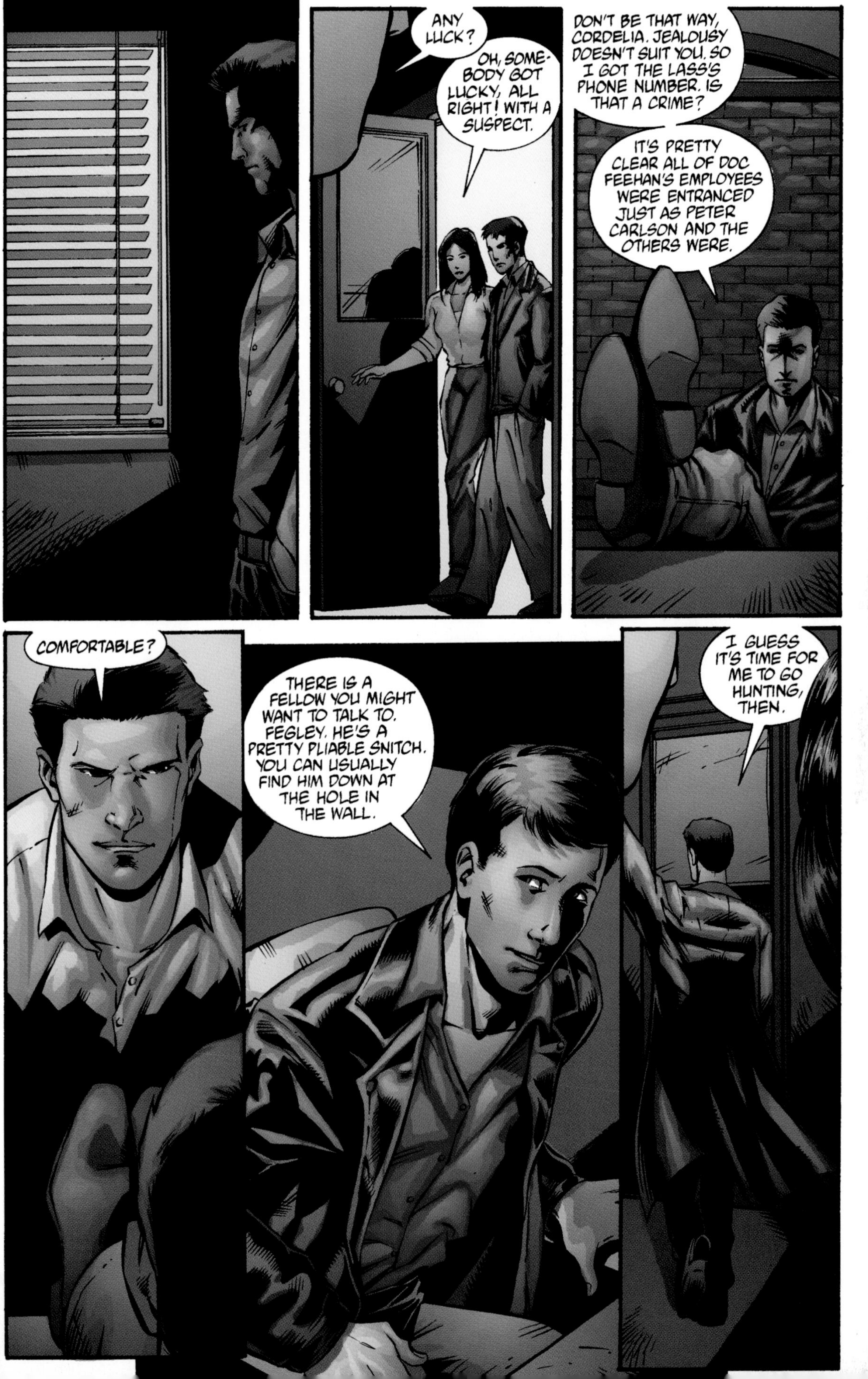
ANY LUCK?
OH, SOMEBODY GOT LUCKY, ALL RIGHT! WITH A SUSPECT.
DON'T BE THAT WAY, CORDELIA. JEALOUSY DOESN'T SUIT YOU. SO I GOT THE LASS'S PHONE NUMBER. IS THAT A CRIME?
IT'S PRETTY CLEAR ALL OF DOC FEEHAN'S EMPLOYEES WERE ENTRANCED JUST AS PETER CARLSON AND THE OTHERS WERE.
COMFORTABLE?
THERE IS A FELLOW YOU MIGHT WANT TO TALK TO. FEGLEY. HE'S A PRETTY PLIABLE SNITCH. YOU CAN USUALLY FIND HIM DOWN AT THE HOLE IN THE WALL.
I GUESS IT'S TIME FOR ME TO GO HUNTING, THEN.

YOU FEGLEY?

WHO'S ASKING?

I'M LOOKING FOR LAVINIA FEEHAN. SUPPOSED TO BE A DOCTOR, BUT SHE'S NOT WHAT SHE SEEMS.

IS ANY-ONE?

I'M RUNNING OUT OF OPTIONS, FEGLEY...AND RUNNING OUT OF PATIENCE, TOO.

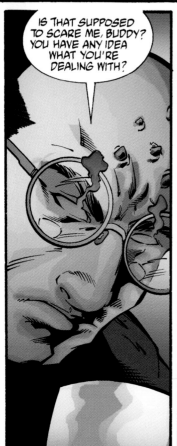

IS THAT SUPPOSED TO SCARE ME, BUDDY? YOU HAVE ANY IDEA WHAT YOU'RE DEALING WITH?

DO YOU? THE NAME'S ANGEL.

...OH...RIGHT... ANGELUS, KILLED MORE EUROPEANS THAN THE PLAGUE. SO...I HEAR ANY-THING, I'LL GET IT TO YOU. RIGHT AWAY. I SWEAR.

YOU DO THAT. AND BRUSH UP ON THE EVIL GLARE. MAYBE CURL THE LIP A LITTLE MORE. NOT ENOUGH MENACE.

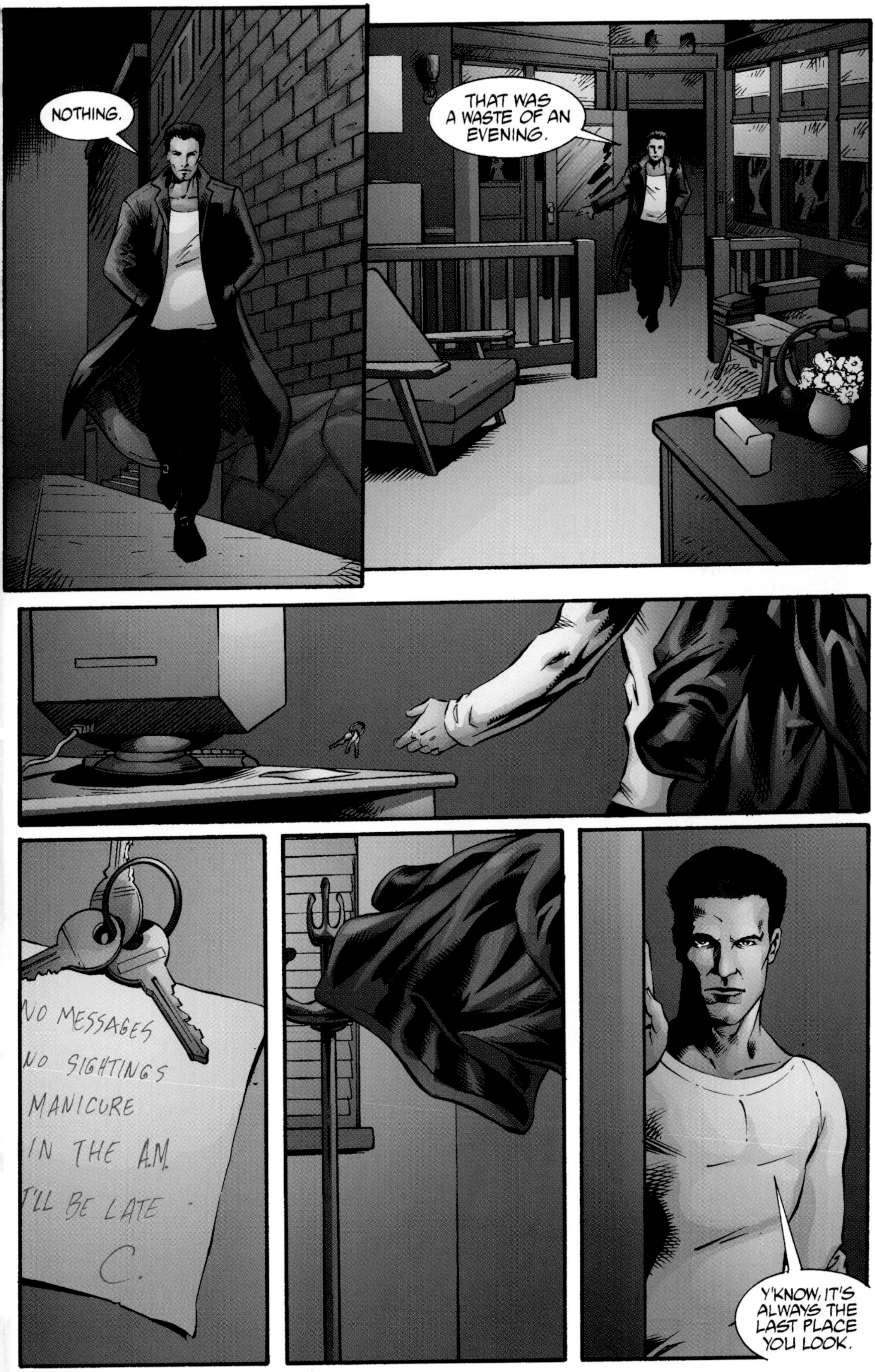
NOTHING.
THAT WAS A WASTE OF AN EVENING.
NO MESSAGES
NO SIGHTINGS
MANICURE
IN THE A.M.
I'LL BE LATE.
C.
Y'KNOW, IT'S ALWAYS THE LAST PLACE YOU LOOK.

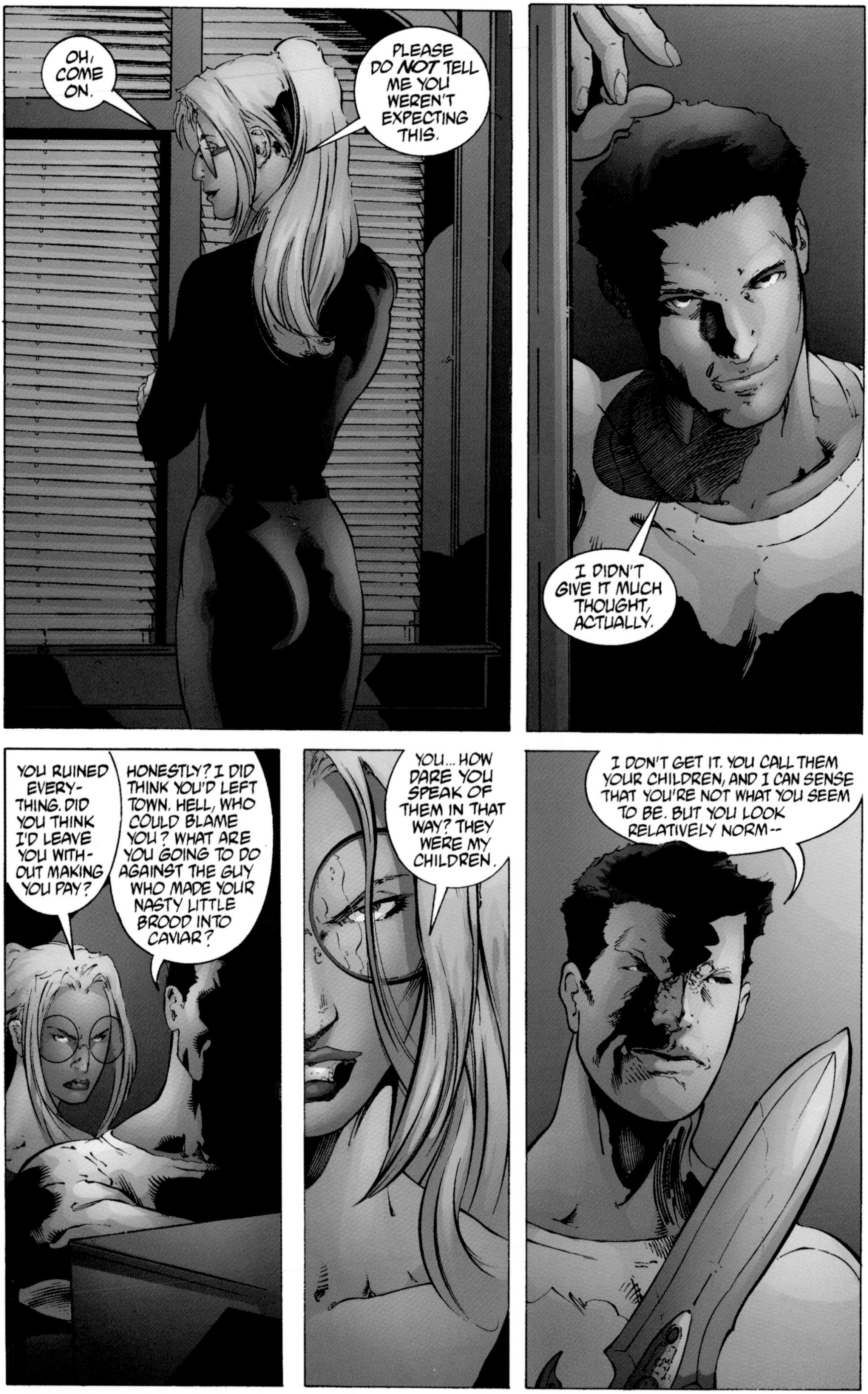
OH, COME ON.
PLEASE DO NOT TELL ME YOU WEREN'T EXPECTING THIS.
I DIDN'T GIVE IT MUCH THOUGHT, ACTUALLY.
YOU RUINED EVERY-THING. DID YOU THINK I'D LEAVE YOU WITH-OUT MAKING YOU PAY?
HONESTLY? I DID THINK YOU'D LEFT TOWN. HELL, WHO COULD BLAME YOU? WHAT ARE YOU GOING TO DO AGAINST THE GUY WHO MADE YOUR NASTY LITTLE BROOD INTO CAVIAR?
YOU... HOW DARE YOU SPEAK OF THEM IN THAT WAY? THEY WERE MY CHILDREN.
I DON'T GET IT. YOU CALL THEM YOUR CHILDREN, AND I CAN SENSE THAT YOU'RE NOT WHAT YOU SEEM TO BE. BUT YOU LOOK RELATIVELY NORM--

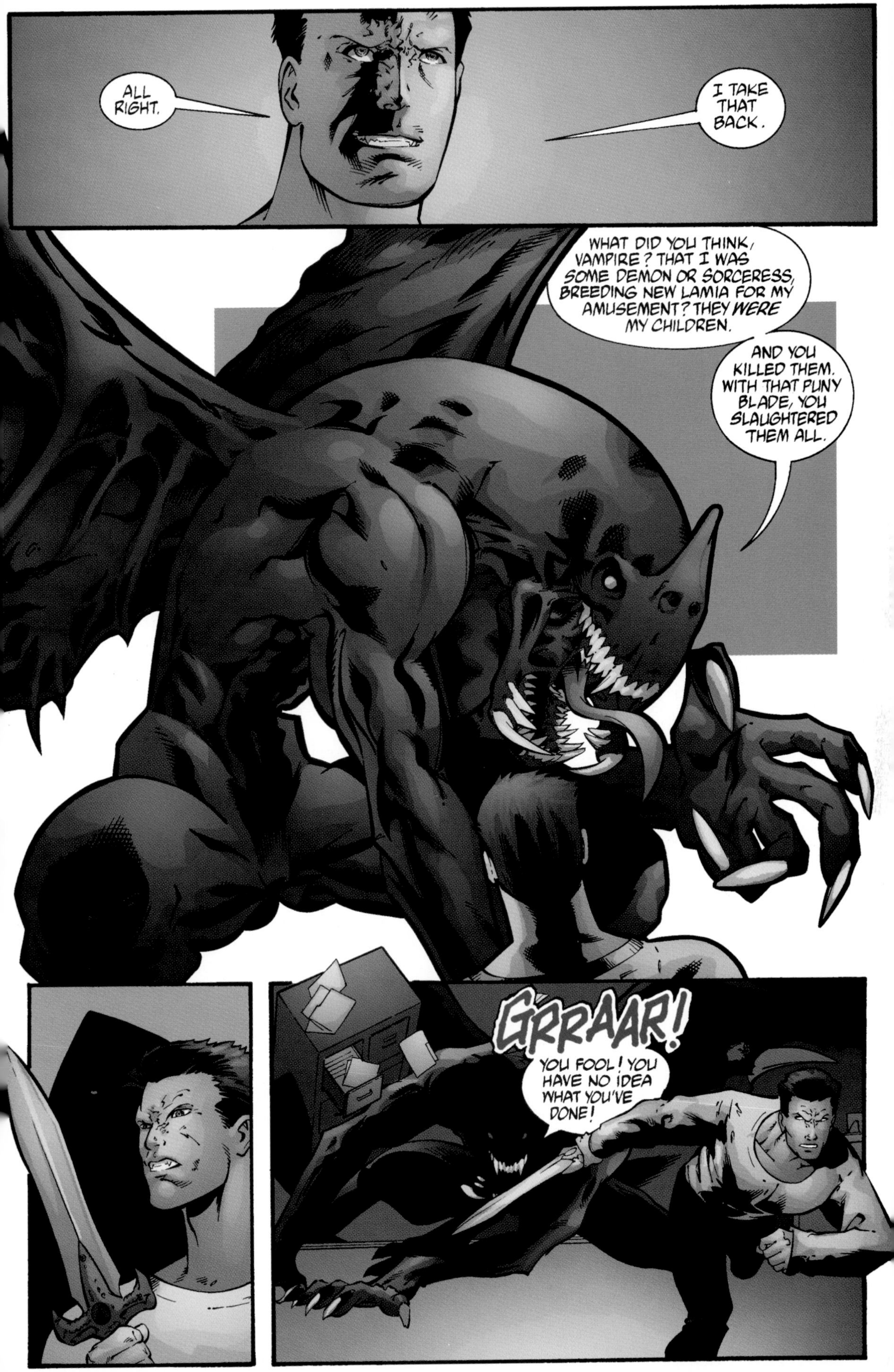
ALL RIGHT.
I TAKE THAT BACK.
WHAT DID YOU THINK, VAMPIRE? THAT I WAS SOME DEMON OR SORCERESS, BREEDING NEW LAMIA FOR MY AMUSEMENT? THEY *WERE* MY CHILDREN.
AND YOU KILLED THEM. WITH THAT PUNY BLADE, YOU SLAUGHTERED THEM ALL.
GRRAAR!
YOU FOOL! YOU HAVE NO IDEA WHAT YOU'VE DONE!

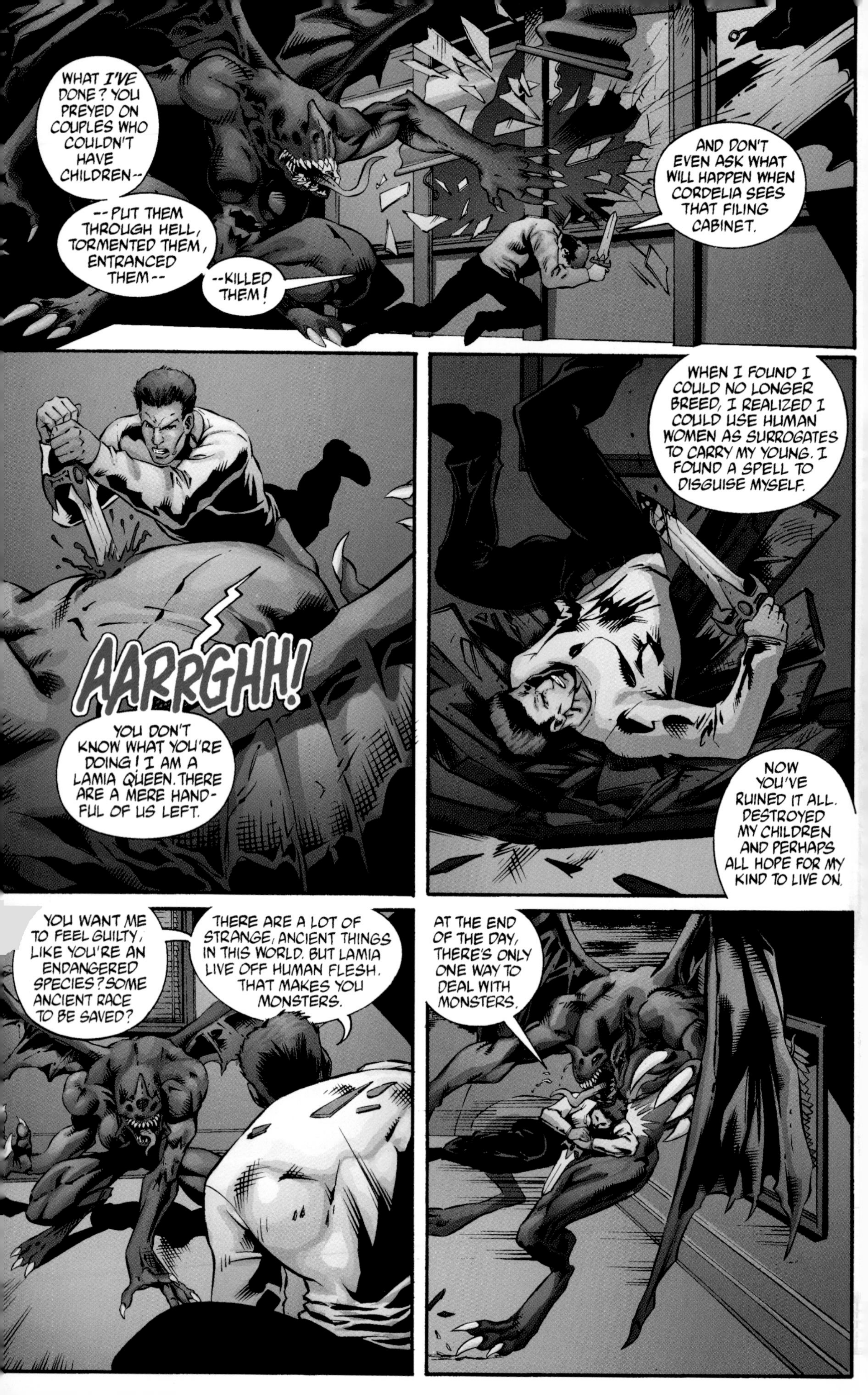
WHAT I'VE DONE? YOU PREYED ON COUPLES WHO COULDN'T HAVE CHILDREN--
--PUT THEM THROUGH HELL, TORMENTED THEM, ENTRANCED THEM--
--KILLED THEM!
AND DON'T EVEN ASK WHAT WILL HAPPEN WHEN CORDELIA SEES THAT FILING CABINET.
AARRGHH!
YOU DON'T KNOW WHAT YOU'RE DOING! I AM A LAMIA QUEEN. THERE ARE A MERE HAND-FUL OF US LEFT.
WHEN I FOUND I COULD NO LONGER BREED, I REALIZED I COULD USE HUMAN WOMEN AS SURROGATES TO CARRY MY YOUNG. I FOUND A SPELL TO DISGUISE MYSELF.
NOW YOU'VE RUINED IT ALL. DESTROYED MY CHILDREN AND PERHAPS ALL HOPE FOR MY KIND TO LIVE ON.
YOU WANT ME TO FEEL GUILTY, LIKE YOU'RE AN ENDANGERED SPECIES? SOME ANCIENT RACE TO BE SAVED?
THERE ARE A LOT OF STRANGE, ANCIENT THINGS IN THIS WORLD. BUT LAMIA LIVE OFF HUMAN FLESH. THAT MAKES YOU MONSTERS.
AT THE END OF THE DAY, THERE'S ONLY ONE WAY TO DEAL WITH MONSTERS.

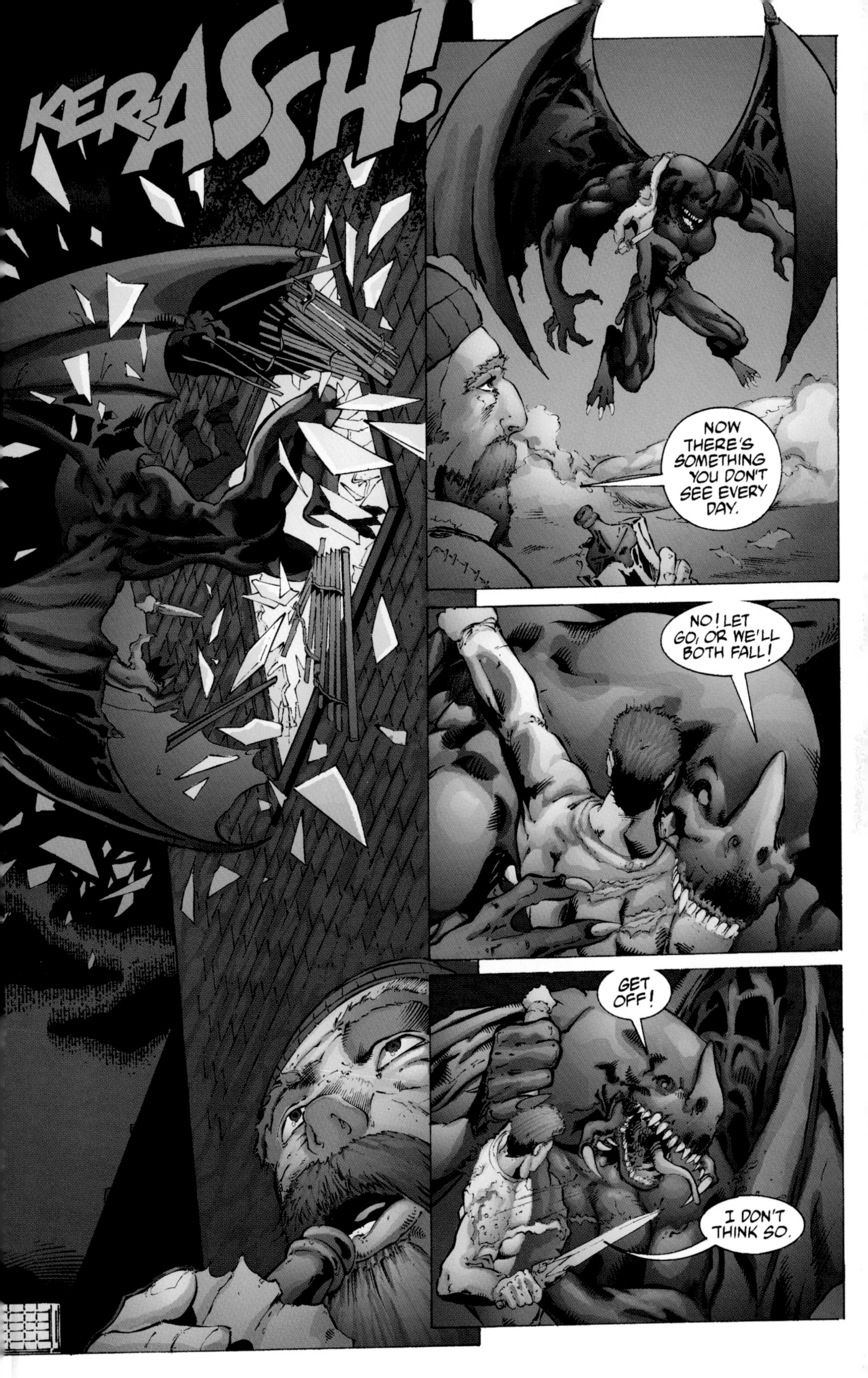
KERASH!
NOW THERE'S SOMETHING YOU DON'T SEE EVERY DAY.
NO! LET GO, OR WE'LL BOTH FALL!
GET OFF!
I DON'T THINK SO.

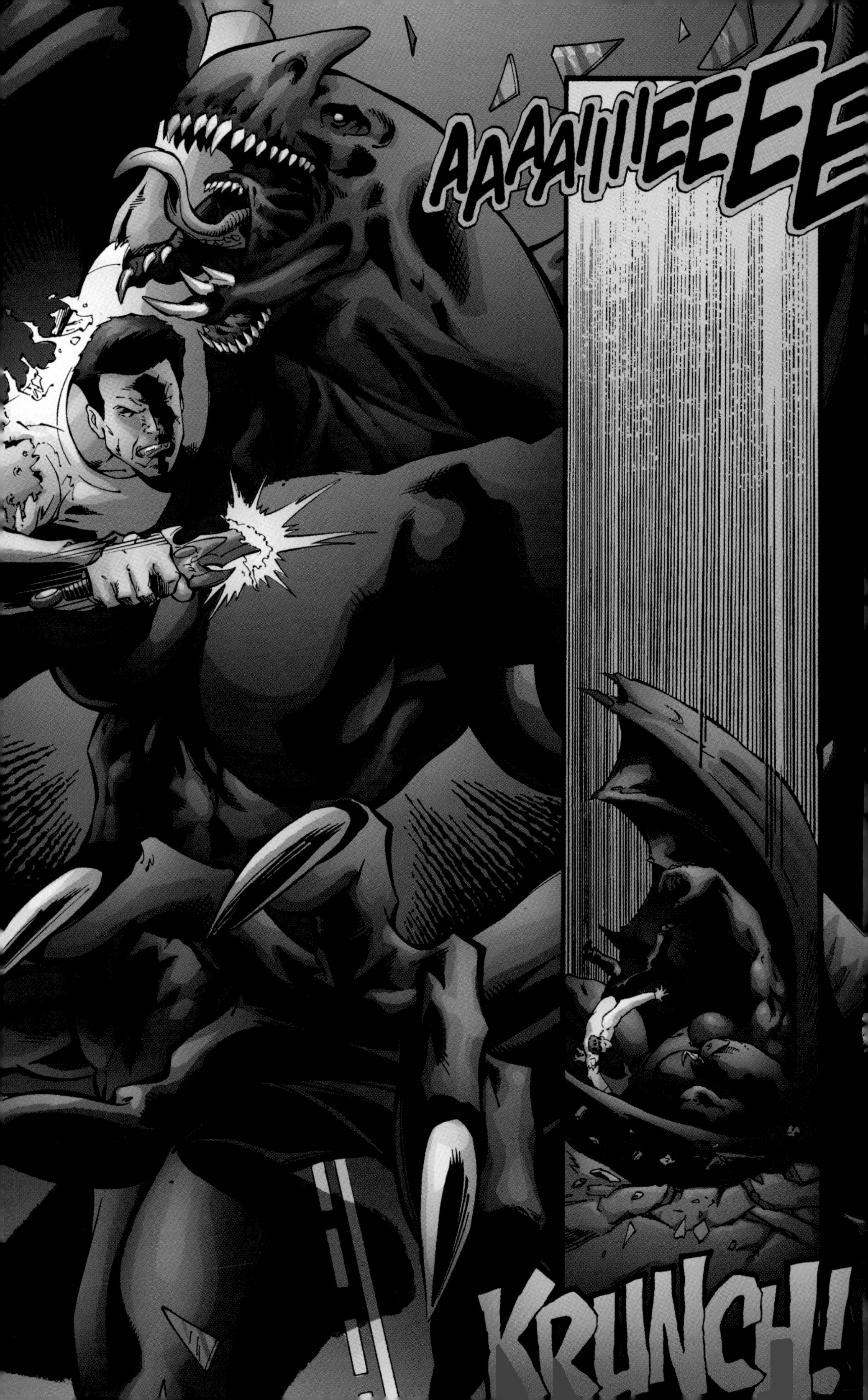
AAAAIIIIEEEEE
KRUNCH!

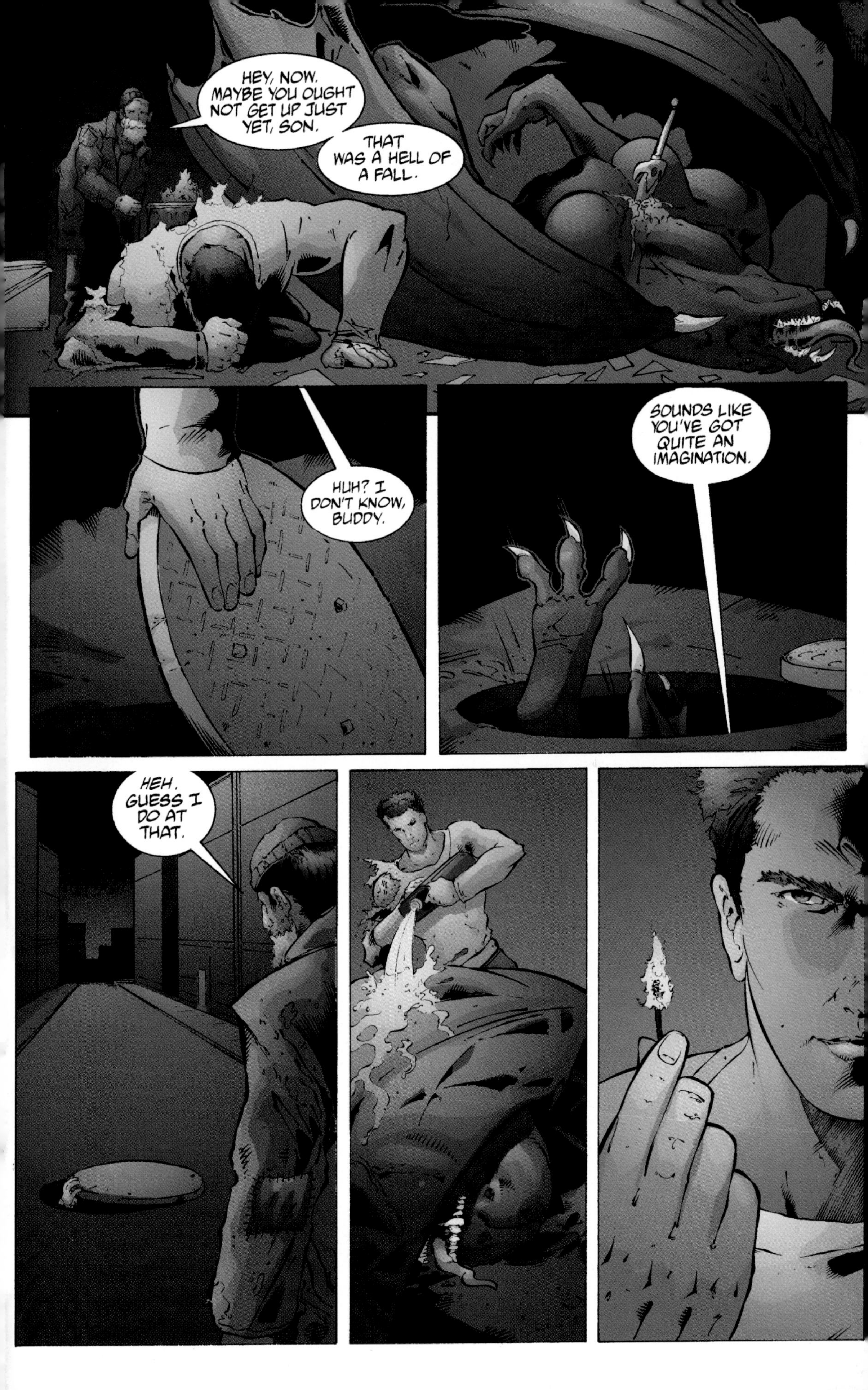
HEY, NOW. MAYBE YOU OUGHT NOT GET UP JUST YET, SON.
THAT WAS A HELL OF A FALL.
HUH? I DON'T KNOW, BUDDY.
SOUNDS LIKE YOU'VE GOT QUITE AN IMAGINATION.
HEH. GUESS I DO AT THAT.

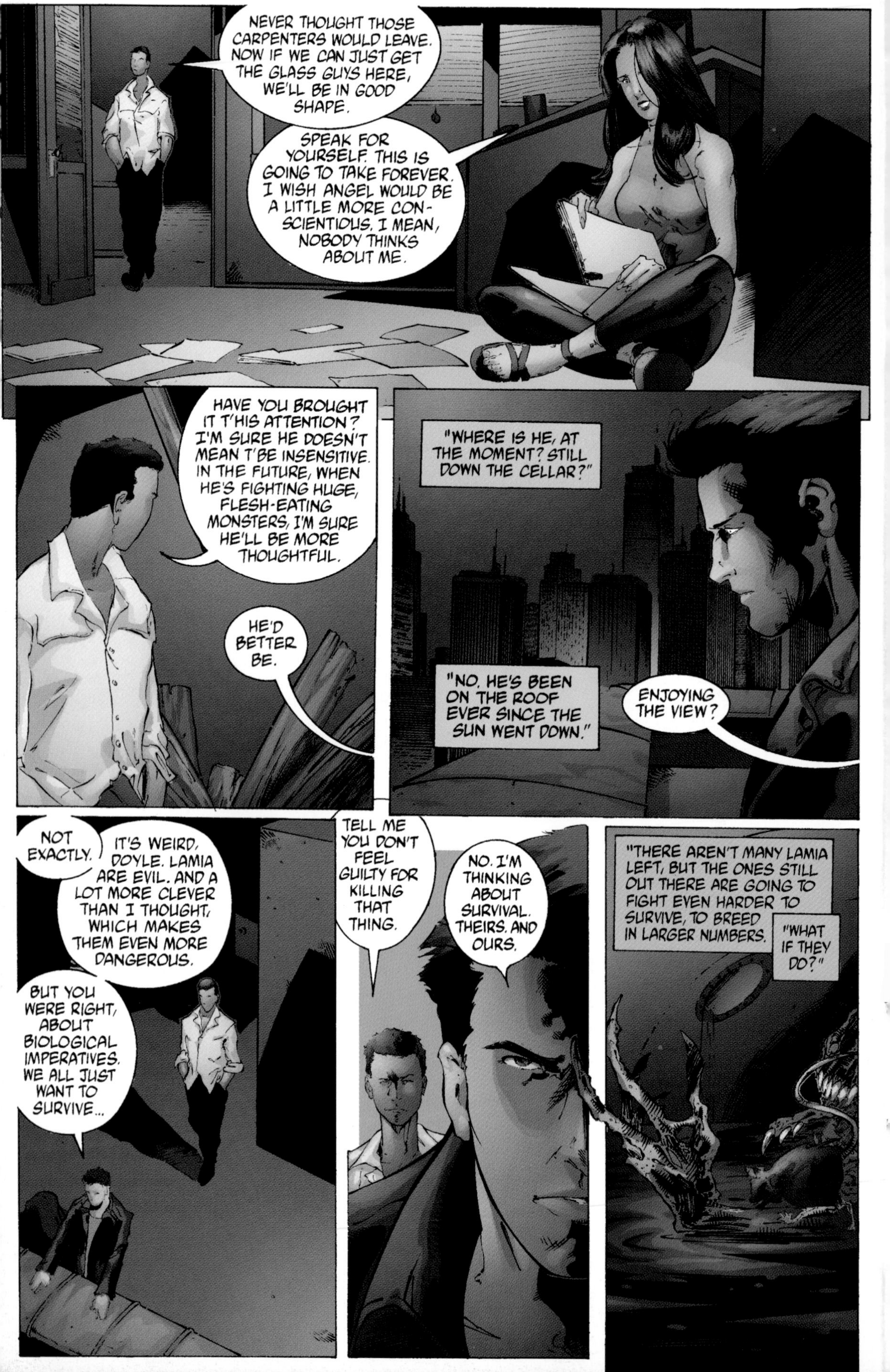
NEVER THOUGHT THOSE CARPENTERS WOULD LEAVE. NOW IF WE CAN JUST GET THE GLASS GUYS HERE, WE'LL BE IN GOOD SHAPE.
SPEAK FOR YOURSELF. THIS IS GOING TO TAKE FOREVER. I WISH ANGEL WOULD BE A LITTLE MORE CON-SCIENTIOUS. I MEAN, NOBODY THINKS ABOUT ME.
HAVE YOU BROUGHT IT T'HIS ATTENTION? I'M SURE HE DOESN'T MEAN T'BE INSENSITIVE. IN THE FUTURE, WHEN HE'S FIGHTING HUGE, FLESH-EATING MONSTERS, I'M SURE HE'LL BE MORE THOUGHTFUL.
HE'D BETTER BE.
"WHERE IS HE, AT THE MOMENT? STILL DOWN THE CELLAR?"
"NO, HE'S BEEN ON THE ROOF EVER SINCE THE SUN WENT DOWN."
ENJOYING THE VIEW?
NOT EXACTLY.
IT'S WEIRD, DOYLE. LAMIA ARE EVIL. AND A LOT MORE CLEVER THAN I THOUGHT, WHICH MAKES THEM EVEN MORE DANGEROUS.
BUT YOU WERE RIGHT, ABOUT BIOLOGICAL IMPERATIVES. WE ALL JUST WANT TO SURVIVE...
TELL ME YOU DON'T FEEL GUILTY FOR KILLING THAT THING.
NO. I'M THINKING ABOUT SURVIVAL. THEIRS. AND OURS.
"THERE AREN'T MANY LAMIA LEFT, BUT THE ONES STILL OUT THERE ARE GOING TO FIGHT EVEN HARDER TO SURVIVE, TO BREED IN LARGER NUMBERS.
"WHAT IF THEY DO?"

An afterword
by CHRISTOPHER GOLDEN

By the time Dark Horse decided to do a monthly comic book based on the new *Angel* television series that was being spun off from *Buffy the Vampire Slayer*, I had already written the *Angel* miniseries *The Hollower*. Apparently the Powers That Be up at Dark Horse liked that story well enough, because they asked me to write the monthly as well.

Needless to say, I was pleased. Great characters come along a lot less frequently than we imagine.

So, grateful, yes, but also a bit uneasy. The job presented us all with certain challenges. With only a vague notion of what the new status quo was going to be for the series, we had to get a couple of plots approved so we could move forward. The idea was that the basic stories would be approved, and as we learned more, and received scripts to read, and perhaps even saw an episode or two, we'd fill in all the holes.

Well, it's all a bit of a blur to me now, I confess, but suffice to say that when *Angel* #1 was being written, we had seen nothing more than a rough draft of the script to the first episode of the series (which was decidedly not the version that ended up on the air). We had the gist, and that was going to have to be enough.

Fortunately, with the aid of *Angel* merchandising queen Caroline Kallas and Fox Licensing's Debbie Olshan, editor Scott Allie and I had a direct link to the producers of *Angel*. They didn't just read the first-issue script we gave them, they went over it with a fine-tooth comb.

Now, maybe you're thinking that would bother the team on the comics. The truth of the matter is, it was a godsend. Since the TV series was only just being born itself, we desperately needed the feedback we received from the producers. I think it helped a great deal in the development of this first story arc, *Surrogates*, of which I'm very proud.

Christian Zanier has done an amazing job of capturing the mood of the series and the characters themselves. Not an easy task, particularly in these three issues, when we had so little to go on. I'm particularly pleased with what Christian brought to *this* story, which had been percolating in the back of my mind for years by the time I got a chance to write it.

Rule one for writers: don't ever throw away a good idea. There'll come a time when you will find a place for it. So it was with *Surrogates*. Way back in 1991, when I was the Licensing Manager for *Billboard* magazine, I started a short story called "Post Partum" that I never finished. It was about a man who comes to believe his wife's hysterical post-partum claims that her baby was stolen from her at birth and replaced with a duplicate, and goes to investigate.

I never went any further with it, but the story never really left my mind, roiling around back there with a dozen others I'll find a way to use one of these days. As soon as I sat down to come up with ideas for *Angel*, it came back to me. Add magic and monsters, and suddenly the story was not only perfect for *Angel*, but worked better than it ever had in its original form. Immodest as it may seem, I like to believe *Surrogates* has a bit more depth to it than your average comic-book media tie-in, particularly for a first issue.

I also think it's really creepy, this idea that the baby you're coddling and cooing to might not be your own. Something insidious about that. I find it chilling.

I hope you did, too.

--CHRISTOPHER GOLDEN,
Bradford, MA, 2000

CHRISTOPHER GOLDEN is the award-winning, *L.A. Times* bestselling author of such novels as *Strangewood* and *Of Saints and Shadows,* and a teen-oriented thriller series whose titles include *Body Bags* and *Thief of Hearts.* He has written eight *Buffy the Vampire Slayer* novels (seven with Nancy Holder), including the upcoming *Sins of the Father.* His comic-book work has included *Wolverine/Punisher, The Crow, Spider-Man Unlimited,* and many *Buffy*-related projects. As a pop-culture journalist, he has co-written such books as *Buffy the Vampire Slayer: The Watcher's Guide* and *The Stephen King Universe* and won the Bram Stoker Award for editing *CUT! Horror Writers on Horror Film.* Please visit him at www.christophergolden.com.

CHRISTIAN ZANIER was born December 27, 1971 and has been collecting comics since he was five. Like most kids Christian wanted to draw comics, and eventually he went to Sheriden College (in Canada) for a year and half, only to discover it wasn't his cup of tea, and quit. He then started his journey into comics.

Along with a few friends, including comic artists Ken Lashley and Marvin Mariano, Christian opened up the studio Draxhall Jump Entertainment. During his time there, Christian met Randy Stradley, who was then looking for an artist to revive Dark Horse's *Ghost.* Randy liked Christian's samples and gave him the job. Ten issues later Christian asked if he could move over to the world of *Buffy.* Randy talked to *Buffy*-verse editor, Scott Allie, and, viola, the rest is history.

Christian is currently working on *Angel* for Dark Horse and *Rising Stars* for Top Cow.

ANDY OWENS was born and raised in Spokane, Washington. He broke into the comic-book field in 1995 as an assistant to some top professionals. After several years of this "slave labor," he struck out on his own. In the past few years he has worked on such titles as *X-Men, Wolverine,* and *Magneto* for Marvel Comics. He has also worked for Top Cow comics on such titles as *Tomb Raider/Witchblade, Ascension,* and *The Darkness.*

In the last year, he has worked for Dark Horse comics on *Buffy the Vampire Slayer* and its spinoff title, *Angel.*

BUFFY THE VAMPIRE SLAYER™, ANGEL™, ALIENS™, AND *PREDATOR™* TRADE PAPERBACKS AVAILABLE FROM DARK HORSE COMICS

BUFFY THE VAMPIRE SLAYER

THE DUST WALTZ
Brereton • Gomez • Florea
color paperback
ISBN: 1-56971-342-1 $9.95

THE REMAINING SUNLIGHT
Watson • Bennett • Ketcham
color paperback
ISBN: 1-56971-354-5 $9.95

THE ORIGIN
Golden • Brereton • Bennett • Ketcham
color paperback
ISBN: 1-56971-429-0 $9.95

UNINVITED GUESTS
Watson • Gomez • Florea
color paperback
ISBN: 1-56971-436-3 $10.95

SUPERNATURAL DEFENSE KIT
Watson • Richards • Pimentel
color hardcover w/slipcase
comes with golden-colored cross, "claddagh" ring, and vial of "holy water"
ISBN: 1-56971-486-X $19.95

BAD BLOOD
Watson • Bennett • Ketcham
color paperback
ISBN: 1-56971-445-2 $9.95

CRASH TEST DEMONS
Watson • Richards • Pimentel
color paperback
ISBN: 1-56971-461-4 $9.95

RING OF FIRE
Petrie • Sook
color paperback
ISBN: 1-56971-482-7 $9.95

PALE REFLECTIONS
Watson • Richards • Pimentel
color paperback
ISBN: 1-56971-475-4 $9.95

BLOOD OF CARTHAGE
Golden • Richards • Pimentel
color paperback
ISBN: 1-56971-445-2 $12.95

ANGEL

THE HOLLOWER
Golden • Gomez • Florea
color paperback
ISBN: 1-56971-450-9 $9.95

SURROGATES
Golden • Zanier • Owens
color paperback
ISBN: 1-56971-491-6 $9.95

ALIENS

OUTBREAK
Verheiden • Nelson
color paperback
ISBN: 1-56971-174-7 $17.95

NIGHTMARE ASYLUM
Verheiden • Beauvais
color paperback
ISBN: 1-56971-217-4 $16.95

FEMALE WAR
Verheiden • Kieth
color paperback
ISBN: 1-56971-190-9 $16.95

GENOCIDE
Arcudi • Willis • Story
color paperback
ISBN: 1-56971-196-8 $16.95

HARVEST
Prosser • Jones
color paperback
ISBN: 1-56971-198-4 $16.95

ROGUE
Edginton • Simpson
color paperback
ISBN: 1-56971-267-0 $16.95

LABYRINTH
Woodring • Plunkett
color paperback
ISBN: 1-56971-245-X $17.95

STRONGHOLD
Arcudi • Mahnke • Palmiotti
color paperback
ISBN: 1-56971-262-X $16.95

TRIBES
Bissette • Dorman
color hardcover
ISBN: 1-878574-28-0 $24.95

KIDNAPPED
Woodring • Green • Lopez
color paperback
ISBN: 1-56971-372-3 $9.95

APOCALYPSE — THE DESTROYING ANGELS
Schultz • Wheatley
color paperback
ISBN: 1-56971-399-5 $10.95

ALIENS VS PREDATOR

ALIENS VS PREDATOR
Stradley • Norwood • Warner
color paperback
ISBN: 1-56971-125-9 $19.95

THE DEADLIEST OF THE SPECIES
Claremont • Barreto • Guice
color limited hardcover
ISBN: 1-56971-182-8 $99.95

WAR
Stradley • Saltares • Warner
color paperback
ISBN: 1-56971-158-5 $19.95

ETERNAL
Edginton • Maleev
color paperback
ISBN: 1-56971-409-6 $9.95

BATMAN/ALIENS
Marz • Wrightson
color paperback
ISBN: 1-56971-305-7 $14.95

SUPERMAN VS ALIENS
Jurgens • Nowlan
color paperback
ISBN: 1-56971-167-4 $14.95

PREDATOR

CONCRETE JUNGLE
Verheiden • Warner • Randall
color paperback
ISBN: 1-56971-165-8 $14.95

BIG GAME
Arcudi • Dorkin • Gil
color paperback
ISBN: 1-56971-166-6 $14.95

COLD WAR
Verheiden • Randall • Mitchell
color paperback
ISBN: 1-878574-79-5 $13.95

RACE WAR
Vachss • Stradley • Raskin • Pelle
color paperback
ISBN: 1-56971-112-7 $17.95

HELL & HOT WATER
Schultz • Colan
color paperback
ISBN: 1-56971-271-9 $9.95

KINDRED
Lamb • Tolson • O'Connell • Peterson
color paperback
ISBN: 1-56971-270-0 $14.95

PREDATOR VS JUDGE DREDD
Wagner • Alcatena
color paperback
ISBN: 1-56971-345-6 $9.95

TARZAN VS PREDATOR AT THE EARTH'S CORE
Simonson • Weeks
color paperback
ISBN: 1-56971-231-X $12.95

Available from your local comics shop or bookstore!

To find a comics shop in your area, call 1-888-266-4226
For more information or to order direct:
•On the web: www.darkhorse.com •E-mail: mailorder@darkhorse.com
•Phone: 1-800-862-0052 or (503) 652-9701 Mon.-Sat. 9 A.M. to 5 P.M. Pacific Time
*Prices and availability subject to change without notice